# I Know Jesus Christ is Real

## King of Kings and Lord of Lords

*A Memoir of Love*

*By*

Melinda T. Deir-Boyette

**Deir To Dream Publishing**
A subsidiary of Deir To Dream, LLC
P.O. Box 20494
Raleigh NC 27619

www.deirtodream.com

Library of Congress Control Number: 2020900219
ISBN 978-0-578-63168-4 (paperback)
ISBN 978-1-7347142-3-4 (audio)
ISBN 978-1-7347142-6-5 (eBook)

This work depicts actual events in the life of the author as truthfully as recollection permits and can be verified by research. Occasionally, dialogue consistent with the character or nature of the person speaking has been supplemented. The names of some individuals have been changed to respect their privacy.

Printed in the United States of America

This book is dedicated to my
Lord and Savior Jesus Christ
and to my mother,
Sylvia H. Leaven (Joy).

*And they overcame him by the blood of the Lamb, and by the word of their testimony* —REVELATION 12:11

*Beloved, believe not every spirit, but try the spirits whether they are of God: because many false prophets are gone out into the world. Hereby know ye the Spirit of God: Every spirit that confesseth that Jesus Christ is come in the flesh is of God: And every spirit that confesseth not that Jesus Christ is come in the flesh is not of God: and this is that spirit of antichrist, whereof ye have heard that it should come; and even now already is it in the world.*
—1 JOHN 4:1–3

I, Melinda T. Deir-Boyette, confess that Jesus Christ is come in the flesh.

# Contents

Faith, Grace, Hope, and Love ...................................1

Meeting Jesus, King of Glory...................................9

How Did I Get Here? ...................................27

"Your Life Will Be Better"...................................41

Please Carry That Baby...................................55

God Does Not Like It When We Worry...................................69

I Made My Bed in Hell, and Jesus Pulled Me Out...................................75

God Is Merciful ...................................87

Seek Understanding ...................................107

Called to Pray...................................111

The Power of Love ...................................121

Did God Send You? ...................................125

My Deliverance Experience ...................................135

Nothing Is Too Hard for God ...................................141

Did I Get a Visitation from God? ...................................151

God Loves All His Children, Prodigals Too ...................................153

I Will Keep Following Jesus!...................................173

King of Kings and Lord of Lords...................................177

Jesus Is Coming Back—the Banquet Is Prepared ...................................181

About the Author ...................................185

# Faith, Grace, Hope, and Love

*Great is thy faithfulness, O God my Father*
—Thomas O. Chisholm

It was June 20, 2016, but it seems like just yesterday when I sat on a university campus in the United States, tears running down my cheeks, amazed by God's goodness and faithfulness. Five years before, I was in Jamaica, having a conversation with God about my fourteen-year-old son Alex going to college. I had known in my heart since he was a child that he would study in the United States; however, his grades were suffering, and I did not see how I would pay for college when the time came. As I sat in the chair, I cried and asked God to make a way.

I felt a rumble in my belly, and then out of my mouth came words with much authority: "Stand and wipe your eyes. Why are you crying? Didn't I tell you I will take care of you?"

I stood at attention. "Yes, you did," I answered softly.

"Move to America," God whispered softly to my spirit.

Alex was in the house, and I knew he was frightened by what had just occurred. I assured him I was not crazy. I told him everything would be okay, that we would migrate to United States, and he would attend college there. My son believed me because he had seen how God had helped us over the years.

To a person with no faith, this may sound crazy.

We knew no one who would file paperwork to sponsor our move to the United States. However, I knew that God had told me to move, and the universe belongs to Him. My sisters and some of my friends encouraged me. They stated that if I said God told me to move, then they believed me. Others thought I was crazy. They had good intentions and tried to convince me that the United States was in a recession, so it was a bad idea to move there.

They could not understand why I was willing to give up everything I already had to venture into the unknown. In Jamaica, I had a job with the Jamaican government, a newly built house in a gated community, and a payment-free Honda Accord. But I heard God, and I was not going to let others' negative comments deter me. I trusted God, and my faith was reactivated.

In June 2011, when the Holy Spirit directed me to move to America, I thought of New York City because that's where my relatives are. A couple weeks later, I received a vision. I dreamt that Jesus took me up in the sky and showed me two states, and he stood between them. One was New York; the other I could not decipher. Each state had a summary of my life's events, depending on which one I chose. New York's statement was one paragraph; the other state was a full page with several paragraphs.

Jesus said to me, "Choose where you want to go. Wherever you choose, you will be okay." I chose the other state. Then Jesus said to me, "You have chosen the difficult one, but it will be worth it." I then woke up. I decided to test the waters. My son and I had ten-year U.S. visas, so I booked two tickets for New York to visit some relatives during the summer of 2011.

When we got to John F. Kennedy International Airport, I was jet-lagged and exhausted. The visitors' line was long and slow, while the US citizens' line moved swiftly with no hassle. I said to myself, "*One day, I am going to stand in the U.S. citizens' line.*"

Immediately, the customs officer split the line, trying to get the visitors to move faster. He called Alex and me out of the visitors' line and said we should go and stand in the citizens' line. We moved to the front of that line.

"Mommy, how come he called us to stand in the citizens' line?" Alex said.

"Don't you see? God is telling us something," I replied.

The customs officer gave me a puzzled look and Alex seemed a bit embarrassed by my comment.

When I reached the officer who inspected our passports, he asked me, "Do you have anything to declare?"

"No," I said.

"Welcome back," he said.

Talking to my heavenly father, using the Hebrew word for "daddy," I thought, *Thank you, Abba. This is my confirmation.* I smiled.

Alex and I returned to Jamaica after our visit. I resigned from my job and sold my car. Two months after resigning from my job, I met my future husband, whom I invited to come and visit us in Jamaica to meet my family. He came to visit, and we were married a few months later.

Alex had attended one of the best high schools in Jamaica, but his grades had gotten so bad that when he came to America in April 2012, he was placed in remedial ninth-grade classes. The following school year, he repeated the ninth grade.

But he persisted, and by the time he was in eleventh grade, Alex was on the honor roll and receiving awards for academic excellence. Entering twelfth grade, he was receiving invitations to apply to colleges, and he also received an academic scholarship offer from a prestigious historically black college in North Carolina. We were honored and excited for the scholarship, but we felt that God was leading Alex to a more diverse university, so he went to the University of North Carolina at Pembroke.

A few months after my son started attending university, I heard that the legislature had significantly decreased tuition to $500 per semester at some of North Carolina's public universities. My son's university was included in the list!

I laughed and said, "Thank you, Abba. I know you did that for us!" That tuition change was God's grace.

God paved our way to America. Today, Alex is a biology major in the university's honors program, a senior scheduled to graduate in the fall of 2020, an in-state student, and a naturalized United States citizen. I am also a naturalized United States citizen.

I was pleasantly surprised when I came to America to find that my husband had a big five-bedroom home in the suburbs. I enjoyed that house, but it was just too far from the city in my opinion, so my husband and I bought a new custom-built home in the city. I now work with the US government in the State of North Carolina. My job is permanent, I receive full benefits, and I have my own corner office. I upgraded my car to an Audi. My husband and I operate our family business, leasing out several investment properties that we own.

Who but God? Hallelujah! Thank you, Abba! God gave more than double what I left behind.

Don't be afraid to start over. Where God guides, he provides (he has already prepared a place). Trust him; he is able. Hallelujah!

Trust him despite your circumstances. For whatever you are trusting God he will provide, if you only believe and have faith. For whatever! Salvation, health, strength, job, family, husband, wife, multi-million–dollar company, daily food, restoration, whatever—God is faithful!

Step out in faith. Fight for your faith. Thank you, Abba, thank you.

Jesus Christ of Nazareth, my Lord and Savior, you are my everything. I love you, God!

*Now the Lord had said unto Abram, get thee out of thy country, and from thy kindred, and from thy father's house, unto a land that I will shew thee: And I will make of thee a great nation, and I will bless thee, and make thy name great; and thou shalt be a blessing: And I will bless them that bless thee, and curse him that curseth thee: and in thee shall all families of the earth be blessed.* —GENESIS 12:1–3

*When thou hast eaten and art full, then thou shalt bless the Lord thy God for the good land which he hath given thee.* —DEUTERONOMY 8:10

I believe North Carolina is the other state that Jesus Christ had shown me in the vision. It has not always been easy. But Abba is still with me. He leads me, he guides me, he hides me, he protects me, and when I get overwhelmed, he sends help!

Thank you, Abba, for leading me to North Carolina. Thank you, North Carolina; you have treated us well. I am thankful. In 2018 I got a promotion, and in 2019 the State of North Carolina recognized me for "NC Excellence in Service" for five years of service to the state. I am grateful to God for all he has accomplished in our lives in this wonderful state.

*But as it is written, Eye hath not seen, nor ear heard, neither have entered the heart of man, the things which God hath prepared for them that love him.*
—1 CORINTHIANS 2:9

*But seek ye first the kingdom of God, and his righteousness and all these things shall be added unto you.*
—MATTHEW 6:33

# Meeting Jesus, King of Glory

*He is King of kings...He built his throne up in the air...*
*Jesus Christ, the first and last, no one works like him.*

—Anonymous

It is incredible, the things we remember: the images, the smells, and the feelings that stay with us throughout the years. I was only a little girl, about five years old, when I first met Jesus Christ. I was a little girl, but I still remember this dream as if it were yesterday. At the time, I lived with my mom, grandmother, sisters, and cousins at Hanna Street, Kingston 4, Jamaica, in a tenement.

In the dream, I remember playing in the dirt of the tenement yard wearing my pink-laced bloomers with no top when I heard a loud sound. When I looked, an angel blew a trumpet; then another angel appeared on the left of that angel and blew his trumpet. Then, what seemed to be hundreds and thousands of angels appeared, one after the other, until they made a runway from heaven to the earth, angels on the left and right.

The trumpets sounded so loudly, it seemed that everyone on earth must have heard them. Everyone on Hanna Street was running and screaming. People were saying, "God is real," and, "It is Judgment Day!" I stood against the yellow whitewashed wall, totally horrified and crying.

Then, through the cloud, came a man on a white horse. His face radiated light, and I screamed along with everyone else as they realized that Jesus was real and that he had returned. Other angels followed behind him, but the man on the horse stopped where I was, and I noticed writing on his legs (which seemed like the legs of a bodybuilder). He picked me up, put me on his lap like a dad holding his child, and rode off with me. I woke up and realized it was a dream.

Time passed. I hadn't seen, dreamt of, or heard the man on the horse for a long while, but I did remember him. I remembered how the people reacted when they saw him riding through the clouds with his angels blowing their trumpets on both sides of him.

Our tenement was near *the two landmarks the Simon Bolivar and National Heroes Circle.* We often played at the National Heroes Park or at the Simon Bolivar as they were both only a two-minute walk from our house. One night later that year, a church in the area had a crusade at *the Simon*

*Bolivar, Heroes Circle.* After the sermon, the pastor gave the altar call, and I went up.

My relatives told me I was too young to give my life to the Lord; I cried hysterically and told them they were trying to get me to go to hell. I cried because I knew that Jesus was real; I had seen him on the horse, and I had seen how scared the people who were not going to heaven were. I thought that if he returned and I were not a Christian, he would not take me with him. I wanted to go with him, to be safe and not terrified like the other people when he returned. I was beside myself. I did not get baptized, as I was not allowed, but I still remembered Jesus.

Growing up in Allman Town with my relatives, I was a feisty child. My great-aunt loved me, however; she told me that I was special and smart. When I was a child, I could predict things, and they happened. I don't know how, but some things I just knew—like if someone was going to die, even though they were perfectly healthy.

Sometimes I looked at someone and knew certain things about them, and they would be amazed. I thought everyone could "read" a person until I figured out that not everyone knew what I did. Once my family could not find a person, and they asked me, and I told them that the person was in jail. They went to the jailhouse and found the person. Another time, I told my mom, "One of your friends has just died," and later that day she got the news that one of her friends overseas had been killed. Stuff like that, I just knew. I later learned this could have been the gift of knowledge described by Paul in 1 Corinthians 12:8.

Ethel ("Aunty") my great aunt, especially loved me. She ensured I never got a spanking no matter how much I misbehaved; she was my protector and was fierce, too. Most people were afraid of Aunty even though she was old because, I was told, she could fight—meaning that she could knock people unconscious.

Aunty also claimed that she could see spirits. We would be in the house, and she would sometimes shout, "Get out! You @#%@#@," or she would stare out the window and shout, "What you are looking in here for? Go away!"

Then she would call me and tell me to come and sit between her legs as if she were protecting me from some invisible force. I would see nothing, but I would join in and say, "Yes! Get out!"

I was confident with Aunty around. I was never in danger of a spanking. Often when Joy, my mom, wanted to spank me, I ran to Aunty. Joy seemed to be afraid of Aunty, so when Aunty told her not to touch me, Joy left me alone. I was also confident that no ghost was going to mess with me—Aunty made sure of that. So, I was never afraid of ghosts as a child, and I'm still not afraid of them to this day, thanks to Aunty.

Once, I got sick, and Joy, her friends, Aunty, and my grandmother all stood over me and did not know what to do. I was so sick and weak and had not eaten for days. My family was so sad, as if they thought I was going to die. But I remembered my friend who rode the horse, and I said with what little energy I had, "God, your child can't take this anymore." Immediately, I felt better, sat up in the bed, and asked for something to eat. Glory to God, I have not ever been that sick again.

My mother, Joy, loved to party and was out all the time with her friends going to the clubs. Florence, my maternal grandmother, who we called "Mama Gigi" or "Mama," took care of my other sisters and cousins, but Aunty took care of me. I was her "special baby." When it was time for my bath, Aunty boiled herbs and bathed me in the water. My bath pan was interesting, to say the least. As my bath water warmed in the sun, she put in a few pebbles, herbs, and sometimes washing blue or a few pennies.

Aunty was a good storyteller. At night, all the children in the tenement yard gathered around, and Aunty told us ghost stories. She knew lots of ghost stories, and because none of us had a television, that was our entertainment. Some of the children were scared afterwards; some of the children said they saw ghosts, but I could not. I tried all they said I should do to see ghosts, but I never did.

I loved Aunty; I still love her. Aunty and I slept together every night on our little sponge mattress on the floor; as she tucked me in, I found comfort in her bosom. At nights I sometimes woke Aunty: "Aunty, please, for a drink of water," and she got up and got my water. One night when I was about seven years old, I asked Aunty for some water, but she did not respond. I tried several times to wake her but no response. I got off the mattress and went to the bed where my grandma and my other sister slept. I woke my grandmother and said, "Mama, I have been trying to wake Aunty to get me some water, but she is not getting up."

## "I WILL TAKE CARE OF YOU"

Aunty died in the bed beside me while I slept and held her. My grandmother called the landlord, and all the other tenants came along. As my family members mourned Aunty's death, I turned my back, because I did not want to look at her lying there. I don't recall feeling sad that she had died; the only thing I thought about was, *Who is going to take care of me now?* I knew that with Aunty no longer around, I was going to get some spankings. (Yes, even as a little girl, I was selfish; it was all about me until I got delivered.)

The other people in the house could not understand why I wasn't crying. I heard someone say, "Aunty took away the hurt and tears from her," and I thought to myself, *That is a bunch a crap. How can a dead person take away my tears?*

"She probably doesn't know that Aunty died," another person said.

*These people are stupid*, I thought. How could I not know she was dead when everyone was crying because she died? (See why I was concerned about getting a spanking?)

I sat on the step, and the man who rode the horse from my dream came and sat beside me. I was the only one who saw him. He wore a long, brown shawl that he used to cover his head and face, but I knew it was the man who had ridden on the horse.

Softly and lovingly, he said, "I will take care of you." He told me that he loved me. He also told me that I would never see Aunty again.

I thought to myself, *Okay, well, if he is going to take care of me, nobody can mess with me, because everyone in the world is afraid of him.* After that, the man who rode the horse in my dream became my invisible friend. He never appeared like that to me again until I was an adult, but I heard him speak to me all the time. I knew that I was loved, and I never felt alone.

When I was about nine years old, Satan came into my room, not pretending to be anything else. It was interesting to me because he never had to introduce himself. I knew who he was just as when I met Jesus. He never had to introduce himself; I knew who he was. I was not afraid, and we had a cordial conversation. When Satan came into the room, he was extremely handsome. His hair was black, and his skin radiated—it almost glowed.

He said, "Serve me, and I will give you everything you want." He told me I could be rich and live in the hills where most the rich people lived in Jamaica. But he never told me he loved me as Jesus had.

I replied to him cordially, "Why would I serve you? We know you are going to lose. Why don't you ask Abba to forgive you?"

He replied with arrogance, "You know I will never do that," and then he faded away. It was strange to me, because it seemed to me that we had known each other long before that time and place based on how we interacted with each other.

## CALLED BACK TO JESUS
### *Softly and tenderly Jesus is calling*
—Will L. Thompson

When I was 32 years old, I heard the Voice of Jesus as I had in the past. In the same soft and loving way, he asked, "Melinda why don't you serve me?" He had asked me before, but I always found reasons not to, even putting the blame on church people, saying that they were hypocrites and that I didn't want to be like them. One reason I held back was that I loved my boyfriend, and I knew if I started going to church, I would have to give him up, because he was a nonbeliever. But, for some reason, I felt this time was my last chance, and he wasn't going to ask me again.

The first time I visited the Apostolic Church (AC), I went to church in a sexy black dress with a split way up to my crotch and one that also exposed half of my breasts. I did not have anything else to wear, only sexy clothes; and that was the only "moderate" dress I had because it was long. I just knew I had to be in a church that Sunday. The people in the church were welcoming and did not pay much attention to my dress; I felt comfortable and not judged.

I went to this church because at the time I heard the Voice, I was just driving past that building, and I heard him say, "Go there," and so I figured that I might as well go there. That Sunday I went with one intention: to wait for the altar call to go up and give my life to the Lord Jesus Christ of Nazareth. I do not recall what was preached. However, as soon as the elder made the altar call, I was one of the first to be up there, if not the first.

The elder finished preaching and came down to the altar and started praying for us. The bishop took the mic and began to sing a song I heard for the first time that day: "He didn't throw the clay away...Empty and broken I came back to him, vessel unworthy so scarred with sin, but he did not despair, he started over again; I bless the day He didn't throw the clay away."

The most amazing thing happened to me. I closed my eyes, and as the Bishop sang, I saw a pair of hands stretch out to me as if they were making me over. Then I saw myself on a spinning wheel, as if the bishop was singing about me.

Then the elder who preached the sermon came over and said to me, "Hold your hand up; the anointing is on you." I didn't have a clue what "the anointing" meant, but it felt good. I felt intense tingling all over my body and what felt like an electric current running through it. I felt as if I had power!

Then I heard the Voice: "I can be better to you than any man." I held my hands in the air and jumped for joy. Hallelujah!

The second Sunday, I went again. I had gone shopping, so my clothes were a bit more modest, though not up to Apostolic standards. As the praise and worship leader sang, "More Than Enough [Jehovah-Jireh]," I closed my eyes and sang. Then, out of nowhere, I screamed. I could not understand it, and I could not stop crying—the tears were just gushing like someone had turned on a pipe.

The third Sunday was the Sunday I got "filled." I was in the worship service singing. I closed my eyes, and I saw myself worshiping in the Spirit with thousands of souls before Abba upon his throne. When I opened my eyes, I thought, *That was strange, but if I were worshipping in the clouds with the saints, why wasn't I up front? Why wasn't I nearer to the Father?* I was somewhere in the middle, and I wanted to be up front. So, I said *Okay, let me see again if this was real or just my imagination.* So, I closed my eyes again, and I saw nothing.

As I was about to open my eyes, a huge presence stood before me with heat and touched my lips. At first, I was annoyed, thinking it was someone in the church with a candle standing before me and that the heat was on my lips. I recalled seeing this big and tall man earlier, the biggest person in the congregation, so I thought it was him. Then it occurred to me that I never saw anyone with a lit candle before in the church.

I had this odd feeling in my belly—it was like a rumble. My tongue started to move in my mouth rapidly, and I could not stop it, nor did I understand what was happening. I began to freak out, but I kept my eyes closed. At this point, I did not want to see what or who was standing in front of me putting this heat on my lips. I gathered up some courage and opened my eyes. To my surprise, no one was standing before me, but I found my tongue moving faster, and I started to speak in a language I had never spoken before—and I could not stop.

After I calmed down, one of the missionaries Sister Francisca came to me and said, "You are so anointed. I heard what you were saying: "Holy, Holy, Holy."

That confirmed my earlier vision in the Spirit when I was worshiping the Lord before the throne. Then a brother Dayton came to me and encouraged me to continue speaking and praying in my new prayer language. Another brother, Leighton, was always there to encourage me. When I told him that I didn't understand what was happening to me, he told me that I was okay. He always seemed to have a word for me whenever I felt overwhelmed. It was also amazing to me because the first day I visited the Apostolic Church, Abba had shown me some people, and these people were among the people he told me I could trust.

## WE WRESTLE NOT AGAINST FLESH AND BLOOD

After my experience many call the "baptism of the Holy Spirit," I also stepped into real spiritual warfare. The enemy of my soul would point out people in the church, saying, "See, hypocrites, they did this or that last night." I would say, "I don't care, it's not my business, I don't want to know anyone's business."

I also saw and heard supernatural things in my house. The day I got filled with the Holy Spirit, when I got home, it was as if I had stepped into a packed house. I could see a minotaur-type figure and several other creatures in the house. I was accustomed to the enemy of my soul and my invisible friend talking to me but seeing things in my house was new.

I thought, *Okay, Melinda; you have obviously lost a few screws.* I asked myself some vital questions to see how far I had gone, or how many screws were "missing." I remembered everything, and I felt great, so apart from seeing these things, I concluded that I was sane.

I also found a Scripture that gave me peace:

*"For God hath not given us the spirit of fear;
but of power, and of love, and of a sound mind."*
—2 TIMOTHY 1:7

But I felt something must still be off—why was I seeing these things? My intellectual mind could not understand it, nor was I willing to accept it as normal. I decided that to ensure I kept sane or at least appeared sane; I was going to make sure to keep my hygiene and grooming at the highest standards. I was a fashionista in my own right. But now I made sure my hair and nails were always groomed. I also decided that I was not going out like a "punk," running away in fear! After all, Aunty had taught me well not to be afraid of ghosts or spirits. I wasn't afraid, and so I said out loud, "I can see you, and I am not afraid—get up out of this house, in Jesus' name!"

During this season, I felt Jesus, my friend, was nowhere to be found. Where was this joy Christians said they had? I thought I must be the only unhappy Christian. Where was the peace everyone at church was saying they had?

My invisible friend had abandoned me. He was the one who had told me to "serve him." Where was he now? He was all I had. He was the only father I knew, the only one who truly understood me, and I felt he had left me.

It was a chronic loneliness I felt. It seemed like I was the child that had stayed home with mom and dad and never went to daycare or kindergarten. Then one day, out of the blue, I was just taken to a public school in the first grade and left with a new teacher and a bunch of children I had never met before. That's how the church felt to me—that I was the weird child.

At thirty-two years old, I bawled like a baby, and I said, "God! You were the one who told me to serve you, and I obeyed, and you left me alone?" I cried, just like a child cries when their parents leave them at daycare.

Then I heard the Voice: "Melinda, you are spoiled."

I was so happy, I didn't care. It sounded like a rebuke, but I heard him speak to my heart, so I was happy! Then I said respectfully, "Sir, if I am spoiled, it is you who spoiled me. You have been there all my life, and now I can't trace you. I don't know where you are—I don't feel you next to me anymore."

Then he pointed me to John 14, where Jesus promised to send the Holy Spirit to be with the disciples. "[God] shall give you another Comforter, that he may abide with you forever; even the Spirit of truth...ye know him; for he dwelleth with you and shall be in you" (John 14:16–17).

I read it, though I was reluctant to accept what I read because I missed him. I just wanted to feel him close by my side again. I didn't want him to point me to the words in the Bible; I wanted to hear him speak to me, to feel him next to me. But then I also wanted to do the right thing because I loved him, so I said, "Okay, thy will and not mine."

One night I felt a dark presence in the house. This had been going on for a couple weeks after I got filled with the evidence of speaking in tongues. Sometimes I got up, prayed, and spoke in tongues for hours until daybreak. One early morning in a clear vision I saw the desert and one of the spirits: what I thought was a "familiar spirit." He resembled a normal young man. He laughed and turned to walk out into the desert from my house. Then, turning around, he said to me, "Don't think it is you that has caused me to leave. I only leave because my time is up—it is daybreak, but I will return tonight."

I stood and I laughed, but it was that kind of laughter where things are so serious you must laugh. I said, "God, this is funny to me. Is this Christianity? I never signed up for this. I heard the lady saying in church Sunday that we wrestle not against flesh and blood but against spiritual beings. But I feel like this spirit beat me up. I felt my body ache as if I was wrestling with someone." I fell back in bed, and I laughed.

"God, you heard him say he is coming back—tonight, right? I am tired, as I have been losing sleep every night sitting up warring. And I know Alex must be tired and scared, too, because I must be keeping him awake with all the noise." Although I enjoyed praying and singing in my new prayer language, I realized that's what it was: my prayer and worship language.

The Holy Spirit said to me, "The battle is mine, and all you have to do is worship me." I was surprised by how easy it would be.

I said, "That's all? And I spent all these nights up speaking in tongues and wasting energy!" I decided that I wanted worship songs that demonstrated God's greatness. I came up with, "How Great Thou Art," "When the Saints Go to Worship," and "You Deserve the Glory and the Honor." I was prepared!

That night the "familiar spirit" came. I woke, I smiled, and thought, *Okay, it's on tonight.* I went and brushed my teeth, and I started to sing, "Oh Lord my God, when I in awesome wonder..." By the time I finished that song, the atmosphere was light, and I forgot about what was going on—I was deep in worship.

Then I started singing, "When the Saints Go to Worship." Satan appeared in my house. I knew he was furious, It seemed at that point he knew I was no longer his agent; he no longer had a hold on me. I was no longer for him, and he was no longer profiting from my sinful life.

No longer stubborn and in rebellion, I had surrendered to the Lord Jesus Christ. I was now redeemed by the precious blood of the Lamb. I became the righteousness of God though Christ Jesus, and God delivered me from hell.

*For rebellion is as the sin of witchcraft, and stubborn-
ness is as iniquity and idolatry.* —1 SAMUEL 15:23

*In this the children of God are manifest, and the
children of the devil: whosoever doeth not righteousness is not of God, neither he that loveth not his
brother.* —1 JOHN 3:10

Satan was not going to take this lying down. "Do you
know who you are dealing with?" he asked. Then he continued
in a condescending tone, "Do you know I can kill you right
here?" This interaction was by no means cordial.

I stopped worshipping. He was standing behind what
looked like a witness stand. Again, he was impeccably dressed
in his three-piece suit and tie, and handsome, but this time
he appeared as a more mature man, dressed in what I call a
"billion-dollar suit." I was not afraid, but I admired how well
dressed he was, I thought, "He is so handsome."

I said facetiously to him, "I did not trouble you, sir, I did
not call your name." But I did trouble Satan: He had lost my
soul—I had truly surrendered to Jesus Christ, and he knew
it. Then I said, "Jesus," as if I was calling for Jesus to help me.

Immediately, I realized that Jesus stood behind me, and
he had always been there. I then said to Satan, "You can't do
anything to me unless you get permission." He faded away. I

had just lived out 2 Chronicles 20:22, when God fought the
battle for the men of Judah while they praised him.

> *And when they began to sing and to praise, the LORD*
> *set ambushes against the children of Ammon, Moab,*
> *and mount Seir, who were come against Judah; and*
> *they were defeated.* —2 CHRONICLES 20:22

Then the Holy Spirit spoke to my heart again: "I now live
inside you, Melinda; the Holy Spirit now lives inside of you.
I don't need to be walking beside you now. You don't need
to feel me beside you anymore."

A few month later, I understood this better when I read
the words of Lord Alfred Tennyson in *The Higher Pantheism*:
"...Speak to Him, thou, for He hears, and Spirit with Spirit can
meet—Closer is He than breathing, and nearer than hands
and feet."

I was happy again—my invisible friend had never left me.
He was closer than I could imagine. I was seeking him from
without, but he lives within. My invisible friend, the Holy
Spirit, now comforts and teaches me.

Hallelujah! Thank you, Jesus Christ of Nazareth, my Lord
and Savior. I thank you! Father, Son, and Holy Spirit. *All one.*

He had never left!

# How Did I Get Here?

*Whate'er my God ordains is right, his holy will abideth...*
—Catherine Winkworth; Samuel Rodigast

In early 2018 I saw a missed call from my eldest sister, Minerva. I returned the call, and she said, "I called you for you to talk to Joy, because Joy is still walking on the road begging for money, and I know you send her money every month, and Marsha is doing her best to take care of Joy."

I started to laugh, and I said, "Tell me, what can I possibly say to Joy to make her stop smoking and begging? All I must do is pray and trust God that he will deliver her and set her free. He did not give her the name Joy for her to live her entire life in that state."

I love my mother dearly, but I have always called her "Joy." My mother was a teenager when I was conceived. I was the second child; my older sister was eleven months older than me. So, when I was born, my mother literally had two babies. My father was in prison for murder. He was fighting his own demons. When my mother was twenty-two years old, she already had three children, and by the time she was thirty years old, she was diagnosed as mentally ill.

When I was about seven years old, after Aunty passed, Joy took us and went to stay with our paternal grandmother, "Mother Deir." Our grandfather, Mother Deir's husband, was deceased; I had never met him.

Mother Deir had a nice concreate house in Waterford, she was beautiful—hazel eyes and mixed race, probably black and Caucasian. She worked at the University Hospital of the West Indies as a nurse. Before we moved to her house, she took us to stay with her on weekends. I enjoyed staying with Mother Deir—her house was much nicer and bigger than the one in the tenement yard, and she had a big standing black-and-white television, and she made the best curry chicken and rice. I loved her, and she loved her grandchildren. Mother Deir soon retired and later started suffering from dementia, so Joy moved us in to care for Mother Deir.

Joy still loved to party, but she was an excellent cook and started to spend more time taking care of us. She made us delicious meals and made sure her girls always dressed up like princesses. Our Uncle Eddie often sent us barrels with food and clothes from the US. So even though our dad, his brother, was in prison, our uncle was like our second dad. When we went to Waterford in the early 1980s, Uncle Eddie visited from the US, and he took my sister Minerva and me to Waterford Primary and registered us to attend.

One day I overheard Joy telling her friend that she wasn't interested in the parties and going to the clubs anymore, because the last time she went to the hair salon, the heat under the dryer was unbearable to her. She thought about hell and decided that if the hairdryer heat could be so scorching, she didn't want to go to hell. During that time, a pastor and his wife had just started a tent revival in an open lot at Waterford Parkway. Joy went and got baptized, and so now we started attending church under the tent.

I especially like church when it was movie night. I also enjoyed the pastor's preaching. He regularly said, "Get thee behind me, Satan. Satan, the blood of Jesus is against you!" That became my new mantra.

His wife prayed before the services. She often prayed for us children, and it was my desire to someday be one of the prayer mothers who dressed in white. During my time under the tent, the bishop and his wife watered the seed that God had planted. Joy took us to church every time she went, which seemed like every night. Sometimes we left and played outside and then returned when we thought church might soon be dismissed.

After a while, I went back to stay with my maternal grandmother, Mama Gigi, and started attending Allman Town Primary school. My sister Minerva stayed with Joy at

Waterford. I heard Joy wasn't doing so well and that my sister Minerva had been admitted to the children's hospital, I'm not sure what happened to her. After my sister was released, Joy and Minerva returned to stay with Mama Gigi, and I was reunited with them after a year apart, while my younger sister, Marsha, was with Joy's sister, Aunty Tuts.

One day I came home from school, and they told me my mother was not home because she had started acting crazy and that the doctors had come, taken her away, and admitted her to the psychiatric hospital. Ever since then, my sisters and I were known as "the madwoman's daughters." Growing up, some people forbade their children to be our friends. My grandmother often said we were "motherless and fatherless" like orphans.

Mama was a stern but loving grandmother, and she taught us respect. She also taught us how to cook and clean, and although we lived in a one-bedroom house, it was always clean and tidy. Mama said, "Cleanliness is next to godliness." She made sure all her grandchildren knew how to use the Genie floor polish, coconut brush, and then the mop to get an extra shiny floor.

Mama was an excellent cook, and she made sure all her grandchildren knew how to cook. She always said, "Whenever you cook, always cook enough food so there is enough left over so that if a stranger stop by, you can feed them." I enjoyed learning to cook, although at times the meat wasn't cooked enough, the food was too salty, or not salty enough, or too spicy, or the rice was too soggy, or I put too much water in the flour and "ruined" the dumplings, or while peeling the green bananas I broke them up. But Mama was patient when she taught us, and by the time I was eleven years old I knew how to properly cook most Jamaican dishes.

To support us, Mama Gigi had a "produce stand in our neighborhood" she would go to the market to buy fruits, vegetables and ground provisions (yams, potatoes, dasheen root, plantains, and green bananas) and then sell these from the stand to the people in our community (Allman Town Hanna Street). Many times, Mama was a great help, because when people did not have money to buy food to feed their families, they could always count on "Miss Gigi" to give them credit on a payment plan for food. Mama had a notebook in which she recorded those who owed her. My dear grandmother loved plants and had several potted plants; the pink four o'clock seemed to be her favorite, as they were all around. She was very beautiful and very proud, and she loved to dress in her pearls. She taught us the importance of personal hygiene and that we should always look presentable when we went out.

Joy eventually went to get our baby sister Marsha from Aunt Tuts; then she and we three girls were together with Mama Gigi. Although Mama was not a Christian at the time,

I saw my grandmother up at various hours of the night reading her Bible and praying for us.

I had heard that my dad was a handsome man, and when I saw him the first time when I was ten years old, I saw it was true. My sisters instantly gravitated to him, but I was reserved; in my mind, the man that rode the horse in my dream is my father. I could not call my biological father dad—it did not feel natural—but I liked him, and I showed him respect. My sisters called him dad, but I didn't, and he did not force me to call him dad either. He called me his baby Theresa, told me that he loved me, hugged me tight, and kissed me on my lips, and I felt awkward: why was this stranger kissing me and calling me Theresa? When I told him, my name was not Theresa but Terry, he looked disappointed. He told me he had named me Theresa, after *Mother Theresa*. He was more disappointed when I told him that Melinda was the name on my birth certificate and that Terry was just my nickname. However, he continued calling me Theresa (and still does, even to this day). I could not understand why people said he was a "bad" person. He was over six feet tall, slender, well dressed, quiet, and very handsome, and he carried himself with so much confidence. He was also well educated. He always had a smile on his face; whenever he talked, he smiled, then chuckled like an innocent choir boy. *Maybe he was framed*, I thought, *and was sent to prison wrongfully*. There was no way that this man had killed several people. My dad taught us these words the first time he saw us: "Good, better, best, never let it rest, until your good is better and your better best." He made sure we knew that poem.

I asked my dad, "How come people say you are 'bad,' but you seem pleasant? You don't have any cuts or scars; neither do you look like a thug." He smiled, then chuckled with even white teeth. He calmly asked his friend, "Who could cut me?" They both laughed.

My family members were afraid of my dad and his friends and since Joy was mentally ill and unable to care for us; my dad said that it would be safe for us to stay in Tivoli Gardens, given his history, Mama Gigi thought she had better let us go. Tivoli Gardens is a neighborhood in Kingston where it is believed to be the center of drug trafficking and where the most notorious gun men in Jamaica stay.

## SENT TO A STRANGE PLACE

There was a man named Dennis who was the "president" of Tivoli Gardens, and my dad told us that Dennis could protect us. My dad introduced us to "the president" and the other men and told us they were our uncles. These men were always jovial, calm, and well-groomed—not even a scratch on them. The people in Tivoli Gardens called my dad a "don," too. Apparently, the dons had a hierarchy, and my dad was right up there with the top ones.

But my dad left us to live overseas the same day he moved us to Tivoli Gardens. We had our own apartment in Tivoli, and our dad got one of his lady friends to care for us. But the "president," or don, for that community was our protector. I liked Dennis. He showed us where we could find him, and he told us that if we needed anything or if anyone troubled us, we should let him know. I thought he meant that he would talk to that person and tell that person to leave us alone. Dennis made sure we had money for lunch and especially on Sunday to buy our ice cream.

I never cared too much for my dad's lady friend because she could not cook nearly as well as my grandmother, and she never allowed me to cook our food. My sisters and I cried the first time she cooked for us; we could not eat that mess; we were not used to that type of crap. Our mother's sanity came and went, but one day she found where we were, so she started to visit us regularly. She would cook for us, and Joy is a good cook. My dad's lady friend seemed to be afraid of Joy, so she let Joy cook. (There is nothing like a mother's love, even when she is not in her right mind.)

One day I was out. When I came home, some of my friends told me that a man had hit our mom. I was so upset that I went to the man that I heard hit my mom, and he brushed me off. So, I went to Dennis, crying, and when he asked me what the matter was, I told him. He was calm and asked me to take him to the person who had hit my mom. He and his entourage followed me.

I thought they were going to talk to the man that I heard hit my mom, or at most warn him. I marched up the stairs with these men behind me. We lived in Building 5, which was four stories tall, on the top floor. When we got there, the man was sitting on the rail, and I pointed and said, "That is the man."

Dennis asked, "Do you know who she is?"

The man said, "Yes, my sister looks after her and her sisters."

Dennis said, as unexcitedly as you can imagine, "Then how come you disrespect the 'don's' baby mother and have his youth crying?"

Then he turned to one of his guys and nonchalantly said, "Throw him off the building."

One of the men grabbed him and attempted to throw him down, but the man held onto the rail.

I cried and begged them not to throw the guy off the building. Then one of the men in the group said, "Bossy, we can't do it here; we are going to traumatize the little princess."

Although I was already traumatized, it seemed to be the norm. But I'd never seen anything like that before.

I begged them to let him go. They didn't listen. I cried, and I begged. Everyone was calm except me. Dennis ordered the guy to follow them, and he got up and walked.

Then, like a miracle, the lady who was taking care of us came around the corner just in time to see them taking her brother away. She threw her hands up in the air, then held her head and begged and cried and told them she was the one taking care of us. They let him go.

After that, she didn't care too much for my sisters and me. Most people in the building were like, "Leave them alone— don't even look at them." Covertly, of course.

For the first time, I realized what my relatives meant when they said they wanted nothing to do with my dad and his friends. That day I also learned what it meant to walk in authority. These men always dressed in business casual, and at no time did they ever appear upset or need to shout. They were always calm. They spoke with authority, and the people listened, every time. They knew who they were, and the people seemed to love and obey them, too.

After that, people's smiles and calm demeanors meant nothing to me—I learned to use discernment and not to judge by outward appearances.

Tivoli was an interesting place to live. I felt safe. The residents lived peaceably together. There were no crimes in Tivoli Gardens, and no one violated the laws, because the punishment was swift and harsh. There were shootings in the surrounding areas, but never in Tivoli Gardens. Children played in the streets at any time of day, and everyone *seemed* genuinely happy and were safe—if they did not violate the laws of Tivoli Gardens, which were basically not to fight, steal, or rape and to respect the dons and their families. Violence was not tolerated inside that community, strangely enough. What an irony.

We stayed in Tivoli Gardens for a couple months. After I turned twelve, the Voice—which I now learned was the Holy Spirit—told me to leave Tivoli Gardens. He told me that he was my protector and that I didn't need dons to protect me. So, I told my sisters I was leaving, and they came with me to Waterford, back to our paternal grandmother's house. We packed our little bags and left, without telling Dennis.

## ON OUR OWN, BUT NEVER LONELY

Mother Deir was old and suffered from dementia. She had a caregiver who lived next door whom Uncle Eddie had hired. The house had three bedrooms, one bath, and a big kitchen, and it was already paid for. I was like a mother to my sisters. I did the cooking and saw to it that my sisters cleaned up the house. My sisters and I took care of ourselves, with the help of God, of course. (I then told all my friends that God raised me.) Mother Deir passed away about a year later. We didn't hear from our father—we thought he was probably in prison or not doing well himself.

So, we stayed at Grandma Deir's home unsupervised. My brother Darius, from another mother, came and stayed with us for a while, bless his heart. An adult, our uncle "Dread," would come and go, often visiting the far end of the island for months at a time. So, for the most part, we were all minors living on our own. Darius and Minerva were both thirteen years old, I was twelve, and our youngest sister, Marsha, was ten years old. It was unbelievable how happy we were as children, though.

My brother went home when his mom came and got him. Marsha went to stay in Allman Town with Joy and Mama Gigi. Minerva and I stayed in Waterford. We weren't going to school then, so I never graduated from primary school, and I missed a year of high school because no one was around to take us to register.

We stayed home for one full year after moving to Mama Deir's house in Waterford. Then a good Samaritan named Donovan, my cousin's husband, enrolled Minerva and me in Waterford High. However, we stopped hearing from our Uncle Eddie soon after we started school, and so the financial support stopped. We later found out he was in some trouble, which made sense, because otherwise we knew he would have been supporting us as he had all along.

At school one sports day I won my race and the head coach invited me to join the school's track and field team. I enjoyed the track team. My best friend in high school, Natalie, had joined the track team as well—we inspired and motivated each other to excel at school, we also goofed around and laughed and made ourselves happy. For me, the track team came with benefits like free lunch, and I got to travel around the island when we had track meets. It was my getaway and extracurricular activity. After a while, Waterford's head coach got a job to coach one of the best boys' schools in Jamaica. Before he left, he made plans for me to get a scholarship to attend one of the best high schools in Kingston and to run for that school.

I told him no, I did not want it—I wanted to stay at Waterford. I thought about the expense and hassle just to get to and from school in Kingston. The coach thought I lacked ambition; he told me of all the opportunities I was throwing away.

I knew he meant well, and so I was not upset at him for being mad at me. He never knew I had no one to support me, and I never felt like explaining my situation to him at the time. Furthermore, running as a career was not my desire—the training was just too demanding.

# "Your Life Will Be Better"

When it was time for my parents to attend school for my reports, I asked my neighbor Joan to help. She represented me, so no one knew who my mom was.

One day, while coming home from school, I saw Joy, and she called out to me.

One of my friends said, "Melinda, where do you know that madwoman from?"

I told my friend that was my mother. My friend tried to make me feel better by saying she was just kidding. I told my friend she was in fact mentally ill, and we laughed it off.

Another time I saw Joy walking on the road, and she was dirty. At times, she slept at the bus stop, even though she had Mama Gigi's house and the house in Waterford, she often walked the streets and slept where she felt like it. I had no one to help her, and I could not help her, so I cried and asked God to take her, because I could not bear to see her like that.

God told me that he would let her live because he was not ready to take her. I did not understand it. *Why don't I have parents, and why do I have to struggle so hard? Why do I have to see my mother walking dirty and crazy on the street?* I thought about it the next day and realized that nothing was going to change. I thought about my next birthday and not having anyone to tell me happy birthday, or not having anyone the next Christmas, and I cried. When I realized that I had no one to comfort me or even to ask me why I was crying, I laid on the dirty floor in a fetal position, and I wept loudly and intensely.

That was the last day I ever cried so hard. I cried until I felt happy, and the Voice said to me, "Your life will be better—never give up." God strengthened me.

I picked myself up off the floor, wiped my eyes, and a joy filled my heart. I went back to talking to Jesus. I got up the next day and went to school as usual. I became stronger—I learned how to deal with the rejection of being called "the madwoman's daughter," and when I saw my mother walking on the streets, it did not hurt so much. I learned to love myself, and I *learned* to be happy and content.

Joy visited us when she could. One evening when she came to visit Minerva and me, she decided she was going to spend the night with us. Joy had a bottle of her medication in her hand as she sat beside Minerva and me in the living room. When Joy got up and ran toward the bedroom, we thought she was joking around. Even though she was mentally sick, she often told us jokes at times. Joy jumped to get in the bed, but she missed. When she fell on the floor, we still thought she was joking. Joy stayed on the floor, then fell asleep.

The next day Minerva and I left for school, and Joy still slept. We came home, and Joy was still asleep. We thought she must have been so tired because she had walked miles to see us. We were just happy to have her home, and so we let her sleep. But after two days, Minerva and I tried to wake Joy, and she did not wake. She just snored and slept.

We decided that if we came home from school the following day and she was still asleep, we were going to let one of our neighbors know that Joy had been sleeping for days. The third day, Minerva and I left Joy and went to school. Because I ran track and field, I came home later that day. When I got there, Joy was gone. Minerva told me that when she got home, Joy's body was beginning to smell, and something told her to throw some water on her.

Minerva said that when she threw the water on Joy, she revived and told Minerva that she had taken a lot of the pills in her bottle. She had been in a coma, and we had not known. Minerva said Joy seemed fine when she woke, and then she left.

Several weeks passed, and we did not see or hear from Joy.

## TALKS WITH JESUS

*Shut in with God in a secret place, there in the Spirit beholding his face, gaining more Power to run in the race, I love to shut in with God.*

—Anonymous

Life was rough, but I was happy. I cannot explain my happiness, but God was always with me, and I certainly never looked like a parentless child. People often asked me what products I used on my body and on my face to make it so radiant: my face was smooth and spotless. I had relaxed my hair; it was thick and healthy as it flowed below my shoulders. My body was toned from the track and field workouts. I was a happy, smart, confident, "pretty girl," and I knew God loved me.

To get money I styled a few ladies' hair on my verandah, and I helped my neighbor Joan with her business. During the midweek, I accompanied Joan to the Sammy's Shoe Store in Half-Way-Tree, where she bought her sandals wholesale, then helped her carry one of the crocus bags as she carried the other one filled with her goods.

On Saturdays I helped her sell onions and the sandals in the May Pen Market. To boost sales, I walked around the market shouting out the price for the sandals and pointing them at people I thought might be interested. Joan paid me by giving me a small stipend, and she bought my necessities.

I could always count on Joan, even though she had her own three children.

Outside of going to school, doing track, and going to the market with Joan to sell onions and sandals on Saturdays, I was usually alone in my house. But I was never truly alone—Jesus was always with me.

I studied and completed my homework on the verandah before it got dark, as we had no electricity; then I locked myself in my room and talked to Jesus for hours. I don't know if it was my imagination or a vision, but even though I was in my room, it seemed as if I were in a beautiful garden talking to Jesus, while an angel stood outside the gate of the garden singing. I could never remember the conversations afterward, but I always remembered him telling me that he loves me.

One day I was in the house, and I heard a lady taunting my sisters, "Is your father's iniquity on you and your sisters why you all are suffering so much?"

I was shocked to hear an adult telling my fifteen-year-old sister that. I was just fourteen. *Why would my father's sins be upon us? I don't even know him.*

I started to cry. "God, if this is true, I don't want anything to do with you! I never did any wrong to anyone. Our dad doesn't even take care of us, yet we are responsible for his sin? You cannot be a good God! How can you be my friend if you put my dad's sins on us?"

There was an old Bible in the house. It had dog-eared pages and some of them were missing. The Voice said to me, "Go and get that Bible." I got the Bible, and it opened to Ezekiel 18. I began to read the whole chapter. Here God told Ezekiel that he does not visit the sins of the fathers on the children.

After I finished reading, I said, "I knew you couldn't be so wicked," and I was comforted.

One summer day I came out the house, and some of my neighbors were surprised to see me. They said I needed to get out of the house more and get some sunlight as I had gotten what they called "house color." So, I went to chat and hang out with my sister and the other girls in the community. I soon realized the other girls and I did not have much, if anything, in common. They said I was too weird.

The day I decided to go chat and hang out was the day they decided to talk about ghosts. Some said ghosts had held them down in their sleep and tried to choke them. One said a demon had pinched her, and she had a mark to prove it. Another said that a demon had raped her. Everyone had a ghost or demon experience, except me.

I told them I never had such a dream or had a ghost experience. But I was eager to share too, so I asked them, "Have you ever dreamt that God spoke to you and it felt real? I have dreams about God."

I said excitedly, "He called me, with the Voice of Thunder and many Waters, and then my spirit left my body in the bed. I saw my body in the bed, and then I went to him and he showed me things and tells me to pray for the people."

They were skeptical, and one of the girls said, "God doesn't talk to people." They said I was too weird.

I was upset, and I said, "You all had ghosts and demons doing things to you, and I don't think you are weird, and I told you God talks to me, and you say I am weird!"

So, I went back to my room and returned to my life as a hermit. To this day, I genuinely love my own company and being alone. I guess I am weird, after all.

## SAVED FROM A WORSE FATE
*What a friend we have in Jesus, all our sins and griefs to bear! What a privilege to carry. Everything to God in prayer! Oh, what peace we often forfeit, Oh, what needless pain we bear, All because we do not carry. Everything to God in prayer!*
—Charles C. Converse

Now and then, when Joy's sanity returned to her and she remembered she had children, she walked miles to come and see us. But other times we did not see her for months. All my friends knew my mother because I always talked about and never denied her: she was "my Joy." Sometimes they told me that they saw my mother on the streets.

One day when I was about fifteen years old, Joy's sanity returned for a while and she went to the Child Services Division and asked them to come and take her girls and put us in a home of safety, because we were living by ourselves without adult supervision and that she was unable to care for us because of her mental illness.

And so, they came for us. I pleaded with the social worker not to take us, but she insisted that we must leave because we were "unprotected." I did not care what she said. I pleaded, until one shouted at me, "You cannot say here by yourself— you might get raped! And besides, don't you want food? And you could go to a top high school in Kingston."

I did not want to go to another high school. I liked Waterford High, which was literally a five-minute walk from my house and convenient. In addition, God had already told me that I was going to college after high school, so I knew things would work out for me.

The social worker was not having it. She saw how we were living without food, electricity, water, or the necessities young girls need in a home. There was no way they were going to let us stay.

I was sad, so I prayed and asked God not to let them take me. I even asked him, "Did you hear how that lady spoke to me?"

The day came for them to take my sister and me to the Maxfield Park Home of Safety. Minerva and I waited, but they did not show up until later that evening. They came and told my sister and me that they had been in a meeting all day debating what to do about us. There had been an incident the night before where two girls had broken out of the home of safety and had been raped, and so they decided that since we had been safe in our home without incident, they would let us remain.

My neighbors came and told the social workers that they had been looking out for us all along. Even the "Boston bad guys" on the street said they had been watching our house to make sure no one tried to enter. Joan, my neighbor, told them that she let us use her water hose so we would have water in our house to use. After seeing all this evidence that we were well tended by our community, the social workers let us stay.

This whole set of events ended up being a blessing, because now we were on welfare, so we could regularly buy our groceries. A social worker also came by twice each week to check on us.

Even though now we were on welfare and had regular groceries, my sister and I stopped collecting the food stamps when I turned sixteen. Maybe we were too proud, or maybe we stopped from shame when a neighbor taunted my sister that we were poor and had to live off food stamps. Either way, I never felt comfortable standing in that long line for food stamps after that. I stopped helping Joan sell in the market as well.

Even this situation worked for my good. One Sunday, I was home, and the savory **aroma** from our neighbor's dinner saturated the air. I was so hungry, and I declared out loud, "As long as I live, I will never be this hungry again." I was determined to make something of my life.

I was sixteen, and Alexander was three years older than me. He was the "cute guy" who lived in the big, nice house up the road. He was an only child, and both of his parents had good jobs, as well as tenants, which gave them extra income. Alexander wore the latest name-brand sneakers and clothes, and he attended a "good" high school. He seemed to have it all.

Alexander became my boyfriend. At first his mom was not having it—she wanted his girlfriend to be of a "better class...at least a girl that attended a 'good' school, a girl who was 'going places,' who at least has a mother who is not mad."

But he decided that he liked me, and no one was going to change that. From that point, Alexander basically financed me, including purchasing my uniforms and books for school. Joy liked Alexander and called him "Roberto," even though she knew his name. He answered and laughed when Joy called him Roberto. He liked Joy, too. She was funny.

With God's help and great teachers and mentors, I did well at Waterford High School and passed the exams. I was accepted to study in a two-year diploma program in

Administrative Management at one of the best colleges in Jamaica, the University of Technology (Utech).

I was able to attend college thanks to our guidance counselor, Mrs. C. Abraham, and the office manager from Waterford High, Mrs. Frazer, who signed for my student loan. My mentor, Mrs. Sonia Glanville, was more than a teacher and vice principal to me—she was a mother figure, loving at times and a disciplinarian at others. Her guidance helped clear the path for my success. Waterford High had been the best place for me.

## A GIRL FROM WATERFORD HIGH

On my first day at university, the lecturer asked us all to introduce ourselves and the school we attended. When it was my turn, I stood and announced proudly, "Melinda Deir, Waterford High." Another student from one of the top high schools in Jamaica said, surprised, "You went to Waterford High? I didn't know that they offered the subjects that qualified students for college." I smiled.

Yolando was my best friend in college. She never ditched me or gossiped about me like some of the other girls did about the things that later came my way. She stuck by me and is still one of my best friends today.

It was none too soon to change the trajectory of my life. I was reminded what I wanted to get away from a week before my eighteenth birthday. A family friend came to stay with us at Waterford, but my sister and I did not know that he was wanted by the police. We were in the house when I heard footsteps on the roof, then banging on the door. Minerva went to open the door, and I ran under the bed.

The next thing I heard was M16 rifles clicking and Minerva shouting frantically, "Don't shoot her! Don't shoot her! It's my sister under the bed!"

Then I echoed, "Don't shoot me!"

I heard the sergeant in charge of the raid telling his men not to fire, and another shouted for me to get out. I came out to several M16 rifles pointing in my face as I was lying on the floor faceup. They told Minerva and me to get out of the house.

The cops left my sister and me alone, but they told the family friend and his girlfriend to stay in the house. For the next couple minutes there were screams from the guy and his girlfriend—the police apparently beat them with the butts of their rifles.

One day I heard that the "president," Dennis, had died. I was sad for him because I loved him. I prayed that he had gotten a chance to save his soul, even if it were at the last minute. He had treated us well while we were living in Tivoli.

It also moved me to pray to God, "Please save my daddy," but, more earnestly, I prayed, "Please, God, don't let my dad die like Dennis and his dad. I want to know him."

I had heard that Dennis's dad had died in prison—a fire in his cell had burned him to death.

My dad got back on his feet when I became an adult. He sent us money, and we talked on the phone periodically. When I was about twenty-eight, I saw my dad for the first time in seventeen years. Most importantly, when I was thirty-three, I got a call from my dad with the most excellent news. He told me he had gotten baptized and accepted Jesus Christ as his Lord and Savior. Hallelujah, Abba! Lord, I thank you for grace!

# Please Carry That Baby

*Love lifted me!...I was sinking deep in*
*sin, far from the peaceful shore...*
—**James Rowe**

I moved from Waterford and into an apartment that was walking distance from my college campus. I'd found new interests and was living my life and having fun. Alexander was back in Portmore, and we drifted in an on-and-off relationship.

During this season, I stopped hearing from God—I no longer had visions, and I no longer heard his still, small Voice. Even if he spoke, I wasn't listening; I was too busy throwing my pearls to pigs. But God did not discard this prodigal piece of clay—even though I was not talking to him anymore, he did not leave me.

I got pregnant when I was nineteen years old, in my final year of college. I found out early in my pregnancy because of the morning sickness. My heightened sense of smell was activated when my neighbor sautéed onions or whenever I went near a person wearing any form of cologne.

With no parental support, no job, no nothing, I also carried a big secret: I was not sure Alexander was the dad. Talk about a triple threat.

A few weeks after I found out I was pregnant, I seriously considered having an abortion. It was in the last few months before graduation, and I did not know what to do. A lady told me she knew where I could go to get the abortion done, and another offered to give me the money.

One night, after contemplating abortion, I went to bed and had a vision. A woman came to me with a basket in her hand. She had a stern look on her face, and she said to me, "God is giving you a son. Do you want him?"

I asked her to show me what she had in the basket, and she showed me a beautiful baby boy in a yellow blanket. I still remember the vision as if it were yesterday.

I smiled, and I said to her, "Yes, I am going to take him. He looks nice."

She gave me the basket with a stern warning: "You take good care of him."

I woke up and decided that I was no longer going to have an abortion but instead carry my son to term, despite the odds. Some people were disappointed in me; they said I was destroying my future by having a baby so young. But I told them I was going to have a son, and I was keeping him.

I also decided I was going to finish my degree. That summer, as I was wrapping up the diploma program, I was an unmarried girl, five months pregnant, sitting in lectures.

## DID JESUS SEND AN ANGEL TO HELP ME?

I was twenty years old and six months pregnant. I thank God for my college friends during this period—they were a tremendous help.

After college I returned to Waterford and found some of my friends had also moved to Waterford, to a house about a fifteen-minute walk from where I was staying at Alexander's house. We all sent out applications before graduating, and all my friends except for me had gotten jobs. I was asked to an interview at the bank, but I could not go because I was so far along in my pregnancy. I wanted to work at the bank, though, because I had always liked to see the ladies in their bank uniforms.

Alexander did his best to accommodate me, but it seemed he was uncertain if he was the dad, so he spent most of his time in Kingston with his "new friend."

For now, I had bigger issues to deal with. When I was six months pregnant, I noticed that the baby had not moved in my belly for few days. Because I had never had health insurance or the money for a private doctor, I went to the Kingston Public Hospital (KPH).

I chose to go to the KPH on a Friday evening, since the baby hadn't moved or kicked the entire week, and my skin color was beginning to darken. As I reached the KPH, a doctor came out to me, which I found strange. Typically, if you go to KPH, you have a long wait before a nurse sees you, much less a doctor. But this doctor came to examine me and immediately told me that I must do an emergency surgery because my baby was dead, and he had to take the child out now!

I was shocked and confused. He wanted to do the surgery right away, so he called the operating theater and was advised that it was closed. Since it was a Friday evening, no surgery could be done until Monday, so he admitted me to the hospital and hid me in the corner of Ward 13 of the Victoria Jubilee Hospital (VJH), in the maternity section.

Ward 13 is where most girls who had abortions and experienced complications ended up. I called Alexander, and he came and brought me some stuff. He was visibly sad to see me in such distress and tried his best to comfort me.

On Saturday morning, I heard someone shouting my name: "Melinda! Melinda! Melinda!"

At first, I thought it was a dream, so I whispered, "Yes?"

Then I heard the shout again, louder and closer: "Melinda! Melinda! Melinda!"

I sat up in bed, still thinking I was dreaming, and I whispered, "I answered you." I thought I was having one of those dreams where God called me. Even though the Voice was different from God's Thunder-and-Water Voice, I still thought it was a dream. But when I opened my eyes, I realized it was not a dream.

I answered more loudly, "Yes!"

Then I saw a doctor charging around the corner and shouting at the nurse, "Who put her here? She doesn't belong here! Her baby is alive; she doesn't belong with these girls! She didn't kill her baby!"

The nurse said she did not know who ordered me to be admitted, because the doctor did not sign the sheet. Then he looked at me and said, "Melinda, you are fine; you don't even need a pill."

He told me that he had been on vacation, but knew he had to come and get me. He told me that he could not discharge me from the hospital because he was still technically on vacation, but he would be back at work on the following Monday and release me then. He told the nurse to take me to Ward 5 until Monday. All this time, he was visibly upset and shouting.

I was relieved and thought, *Saved by the bell*—until this old nurse with nails like a bird's claws came into Ward 5 and started cursing at me and told me my baby was dead and that they were going to take it out. The girl in the bed beside me asked why the nurse was treating me so harshly. I told her I didn't know.

I was sad, and I got angry at God. I said, "Why are you allowing this to happen to me? I never aborted my baby, but if I had, I wouldn't be going through all of this."

I continued, "All my friends have jobs and are living their lives, and I chose to have my baby. If you knew my baby was going to die, why did you let me continue with this pregnancy for six months?"

Then, in a sweet and loving voice, I heard God say, "Melinda, that is the wrong attitude."

I didn't know anything about repenting, because I was not yet a Christian, nor did I attend church, so I said, "I am sorry"—and I was genuinely sorry. Then I said, "I want my baby."

Immediately, I felt the baby move, and he went on to kick all night. The other girls in the ward were happy for me, and they all came and touched my stomach and joked that my baby wanted to live because he had started to move. God renewed my strength, and I felt better.

Early on Monday, the same nurse entered and said that she had come to take me to the operating theater to do the surgery. I told her that my baby was alive.

The lady started to curse me again, and she tried to get closer to get me out the bed.

This time I perceived that she and the doctor that admitted me to the hospital were agents of the devil. I believed she was a witch, so I spoke to her spirit: "If you touch me again, I will break every bone in your hand."

She realized that I knew who she was, and she immediately backed away, but she was still cursing me, calling me the worst names you could call a woman. But nothing she said upset me because God had given me extra strength. Glory to God!

## HE CARES FOR YOU

I was released from the hospital that day because the good doctor had returned to work, God bless him. (I still need to call VJH and find him.) He told me that because I had been admitted to VJH, I now had to attend their prenatal clinic.

Alexander brought me home from the hospital, dropped me off at his house, and left. Feeling alone, I could not sleep, so I prayed. I have never forgotten that prayer.

"God, I am not going to worry anymore, and I am not going to cry either. The doctor said I needed to rest, so I am going to sleep now. Okay. You know I must start the clinic at VJH, and you see that they are trying to kill my baby and me; I just don't want to go down there by myself. I will talk to you tomorrow, okay. Goodnight."

As I finished praying, the house phone rang. I answered, and the person asked for a strange name I had never heard before. I laughed and said, "You have the wrong number."

"No, I don't," the person said. "Anyway, what are you doing up so late?"

I proceeded to tell him that I was pregnant and that I had been released from the hospital and now had to go to the weekly clinic.

The man said, "As long as you must go down there, I will follow you."

I started to laugh. "You don't even know me," I told him, "and you don't even know if I am telling the truth about being pregnant."

He simply said, "When I see you, I will know if you are pregnant, and everything else, I will know if it is true eventually."

I laughed and concurred.

I said he couldn't follow me because I had to go every week and sometimes twice per week.

"Not a problem," he said. "I only work at night, so I can spend every day with you if I want to."

I asked him his name and what work he did. He said his name was Michael and that he was in the security business. I told him my name is Terry (my nickname) and when my next clinic appointment was. Then I hung up the phone and went to bed.

On my next prenatal clinic appointment day, I heard the phone ring at 5:00 a.m. I answered and heard a soft voice say, "Terry, this is Michael. Remember, you have an appointment today."

I was surprised that he had remembered, and I asked if he was going to follow me. He said he would go by the clinic and collect a number for me so I could see the doctor quickly. He described himself and what he was wearing.

When I went to KPH, I saw a tall, dark, handsome man in his mid-thirties, dressed in white trousers and a white shirt, waiting for me.

The first thought I had was that this man did not have a sense of style, but I was grateful he was there, and I thanked him. I also thought it was weird that he didn't have a girl-friend, wife, or children.

I attended the VJH prenatal clinic from September through November 1996, and Michael was always there with me.

As the weeks went by, I found it strange that he never once asked me any pertinent questions or even told me that I was a nice girl.

When I asked him why he never tried to make a pass at me, he said, "I am just here to help you. I am here to make sure you are okay," so I thought he was just a nice guy.

But when I was nine months pregnant, I began to feel concerned that this man was just too weird. Maybe he wanted to steal my baby or something. I just could not understand why he was so nice to me without expecting anything in return. He gave me money and sat with me for hours in the public clinic. He called me and kept me company at night, and he never once seemed irritated or made me feel as if he was doing me a favor or that I owed him anything. He even went to the blood bank and gave blood for me.

Then one day, he said to me, "I have never touched a pregnant woman before. Can I touch your belly?" I said, "Sure," but when he touched me, he hastily removed his hand as if he had just put it in the coals of a fire.

*This man is too weird*, I thought.

I wanted other people to know him and help me decide if I should trust him, but he only met me at the hospital, followed me to the bus stop, made sure I got a seat on the bus, and then left. None of my friends ever met him.

One day, on my last clinic visit before I had my baby, he said, "I am going to follow you home today."

I was happy and started to tell him all the thoughts that were going through my head. I shared how I was worried that he wanted to steal my baby. I asked why he was so nice to me.

He asked me, "How do those thoughts come to your mind?" He never seemed to understand my thoughts.

He came home with me and spent the entire day there, staying until I was ready for bed. I introduced him to my sister Minerva and my neighbor, and I felt better. If he tried to steal my baby, at least I had other people who could identify him. That was the last time I saw Michael for a couple weeks.

The next day, I was feeling a little discomfort, and I went to the Victoria Jubilee Hospital to have my son. The doctor "broke my water," but I was not having labor pains. After giving me two bags of IVs, the doctors told me that if I wasn't in labor soon, a Cesarean section was the next option.

I did not want that; my mind went to the doctor and the nurse who had wanted to take my baby at six months. It was as if I could see them in my mind's eye, waiting for me in the operating theater. So, I went into the labor ward and started pushing.

A nurse I saw there told me that I was not fully dilated, so I should not be pushing. She gave me an injection in my leg, put me in a bed, pulled up the railing, and told me not to get out the bed, because the medication she gave me was going to make me drowsy and fall asleep. Even if I wanted to use the restroom, I should go in the bed, and someone would clean it up.

I was awakened by the urge to use the restroom, and I started to push. My son came into the world on a Saturday, ten minutes past eight o'clock on November 30, 1996. When the baby was born, he looked exactly like the baby in the basket in my vision, and I knew he was Alexander's child. God is faithful!

I thanked Jesus Christ for several minutes while I laid on the bed after giving birth. I did not experience labor pains as the injection I had gotten earlier had numbed me. Hallelujah!

The day I took the baby home, one of my neighbors gave me two huge bags of baby clothes. She said her sister was in America and had sent some things for her family, including those bags, which she had told her to give to someone she knew with a baby. While I was pregnant, God had someone baby shopping for me. Hallelujah!

My friend Paulette also gave me some baby stuff and unique baby bottles and other items that she had received from her family in America. Another friend, Criscia, and her grandmother helped me take care of my baby. God provided in every way!

A few weeks passed, and I had mostly forgotten about my new friend Michael. When I remembered him, I called his phone, excited to talk with him. I told him that I had the baby, and I wanted to make him the godfather. He was going to love my baby because he was so cute!

I was so excited, but Michael seemed distant. I asked, "Don't you want to see the baby? I want you to meet my baby."

He asked me to hold for a minute, as if he had to ask permission from someone to come and see me. I knew he was weird and all, but this was just crazy.

He came back to the phone and told me that he could come and see me, but only a few minutes, because he had to work.

I was puzzled. Before, he could spend all his time with me, but now he couldn't?

I agreed to his short visit.

He came and stayed for less than five minutes. I asked if he wanted to hold the baby. He said no. I followed him to the bus stop. The next day I called his phone and got a recording:

"We're sorry, but the number you are calling is no longer in service." It has been twenty-four years, and I have not seen or heard from Michael since.

I pray whenever I think of Michael. If he was an angel, I thank God for sending him and ask God to please tell him thanks for me. If he was just a man and is still alive somewhere, I pray that he is okay; and if he is no longer alive, I pray that he found comfort in Jesus' arms.

Father, I have not been a perfect mother, but I have done the best I could to take care of the son you blessed me with. I was a good custodian. Now, righteous Father, I give him back to you. I cannot love him and care for him as you can.

He is currently a man and out of my house, in college and on his own. But I know he is never alone because you are always with him, and I thank you. You are the greatest Father.

Father, please draw him back to you. Holy Father, please speak to him clearly as you did when he was a child and let him walk in your ways. I give you all the honor and glory. In Jesus' name, I pray. Amen!

Thank you, Abba. Glory to God in the highest. My children will be great in this nation! The Lord will teach my children, and great will be their peace. Hallelujah.

> *All thy children shall be taught of the Lord; and great shall be the peace of thy children. This is the heritage of the servants of the Lord, and their righteousness is of me, saith the Lord.* —ISAIAH 54:13, 17

I cannot judge a woman for having an abortion. I know the distress of seriously considering it and how dim the future looks when you can't see a clear path. I don't know what it is like to have an abortion, but I can imagine the distress of wondering what might have been or what that child might have looked like. If it were not for that dream, maybe I would have known this pain.

If you have had one, God can forgive you, so trust that he has. If you are reading this message and are contemplating abortion, believe God! Please carry that baby—God will help you! I won't tell you it is going to be easy, but God will help you. He has helped me mightily—I am a witness!

# God Does Not Like It When We Worry

*Why should I feel discouraged?*
*Why should the shadows come?*
—Civilla D. Martin

I was twenty-one, going on twenty-two. I was about to be made redundant at my job, and they were closing the company. I had a baby boy to feed and care for, and Alex's dad had been made redundant at his job in the same month, so he had no way of providing for us.

I was so stressed out. How was I going to provide for myself and my baby boy? He was going to need diapers and food, at least. I needed to take care of myself and pay my bills. I was worried!

One night after I'd gone to bed, I wasn't sure when I fell asleep, but I heard the Voice of Thunder and Water calling me: "Melinda, come here!"

By now, I knew the routine. I saw my spirit leave my body, and I went to *him*. Clouds and thick darkness surrounded him. I fell on my face to worship him, but this time the scene was different.

Two men were standing at attention—one on my left, the other on my right. I recognized one of the men. He resembled Michael—the man who came to my aid when I was pregnant, whom I had never seen again until that moment. But Michael acted as if he never knew me. I also found it strange that Michael and the other person could stand in that remarkable presence, because I had difficulty even staying alive.

I prostrated myself with the intent to worship when I heard the Voice of Thunder and Water say to me, "No, don't. Stand!"

*Nobody can stand before this*, I thought. *If I stand, I am going to die.*

In the spirit, everyone can read each other's thoughts, it seems, because Michael looked at me and said sternly, "Melinda, if he tells you to stand, you stand." He then stood at attention, as if he had never seen me a day before in his life.

At that moment, I learned my first lesson: You have no friends in the spiritual world unless God considers you his friend. If you are a person (such as a witch or a warlock) who thinks you can control demons, you don't—they control you, and they hate you with a passion. They only pretend you can control them; they are lying to you. They are the same ones who will drag your soul to hell and will even hurt you physically while you are alive.

If angels sent from the Lord Jesus Christ assisted you, it was not you who summoned them—they only do what Abba tells them. No one can order angels or demons around; they only do what their master commands. They operate like a real army and follow their captain and commander-in-chief only.

> And it came to pass, when Joshua was by Jericho, that he lifted up his eyes and looked, and, behold, there stood a man over against him with his sword drawn in his hand: and Joshua went unto him, and said unto him, Art thou for us, or for our adversaries? And he said, Nay; but as captain of the host of the Lord army, I now come. And Joshua fell on his face to the earth, and did worship, and said unto him, What saith my lord unto his servant?
> —JOSHUA 5:13–14

So, I spoke to the angel Michael through telepathy. I was upset with him; I had thought he was my friend. He looked like my friend, but he ignored me, so I said, "Well, if you are going to pretend you don't know me, I am not going to let it bother me." (Though it did.)

I said to "Michael", "If you can stand in this, then I can stand, too; I am a soldier like you."

Then I forced myself to stand, and I said to myself, *Melinda, make sure you don't fall on your face. You must remain standing because you see that you have gotten me into enough trouble.* It was weird—I knew my body was in bed, back in the house, but I was talking to another part of me.

So, I stood like a soldier at attention, just like Michael. Nothing I said affected him in any way; he just stood at attention.

Then the Voice of Thunder and Water said, "Melinda, why are you worrying? Don't you trust me? Didn't I tell you I will take care of you?"

I learned my second lesson: Worry is a sin. It means that you don't believe the one true God. It means you have no faith in God, and you believe the devil. It means that you take God as a liar.

> *"For whatsoever is not of faith is sin."* —ROMANS 14:23

I said, "I trust you."

Then I thought, *I don't remember him telling me that he will take care of me, but if he said it, it must mean that I don't remember, because I know he cannot lie.*

(I later recalled that he did tell me that when I was a little girl.)

So I said, "Yes! You did say all those things."

I was about to fall on my face because the glory was just too great to stand in.

As I was about to fall, the Voice of Thunder and Water said to me, "Hold up your hands."

I held up my hands. A little piece of the cloud moved, and the brightest light you can imagine started to shine down on me. The light was like liquid honey but neither sticky nor thick. The light had musical notes in it, and the light was alive...It was just incredible. I cannot describe it fully.

The light touched the tips of my fingers and went straight through my entire body; I could not contain it. Then I shouted, "God!"

"Yes," he answered.

I told him that my boss was a good man and that he was going to lose his job as well and that he had a family. I asked if God could give him some of this light, too. Instantly I saw my boss at his desk, and the light found him and penetrated him. He jumped up and started to praise God! I knew it was real. (He is now a full-time pastor.)

I woke up with the sun shining in my face. I was sweating and saying, "I am not going to worry again," over and over.

God is faithful; he provides for my boy and for me. I now have two boys, glory to God—God has always been faithful to me. Every time I start to worry, I remember this dream as if it were yesterday. God doesn't like it when we worry, because then we believe the lies of the enemy instead of having faith and believing the one true God, Jehovah, the Father of our Lord and Savior Jesus Christ.

Believe Jesus—believe God—have faith. Jesus Christ is real, and he will help you! I tried it, and it works. Faith works!

# I Made My Bed in Hell, and Jesus Pulled Me Out

*Depth of mercy! Can there be mercy still reserved for me? ...I have long withstood His grace: long provoked Him to His Face*
—**Charles Wesley**

God showed me his mercy when I was in relations that were not ordained for me. I had become heartbroken, distressed, oppressed, and obsessed. Alexander and I had broken up, and during this time our son, Alex, stayed with me during the week, and on the weekend, he stayed with his dad.

Karen, one of my best friends from college, was also my roommate. She looked out for me. All my friends from college had gotten good jobs, but I only worked contracted jobs with low pay. I had a conversation with God as to why I was unable to get a good job or why things were not working out for me.

That same Sunday, Karen returned from a church she had visited for the first time. Laughing hysterically, she said: "Mel, I had the weirdest experiences at a church. Firstly, the lady threw water on me, then she threw a coconut over my head and broke it on the wall and then screamed in my ear."

Karen proceeded to scream the words in my ear: "Seek ye first the kingdom of God and his righteousness and all these things shall be added on to you!".

Karen continued to laugh and said, "Mel, don't you see these people are crazy? What kind of church is that?"

I laughed with her, but I knew that the message was for me. It was the answer to the question I had asked God earlier.

I was about twenty-three years old when I met Eric. I especially loved his mind. We talked for hours about everything and nothing. He is an intellect, a great orator, and an English professor, but he left the teaching profession to work as a radio and TV presenter. He soon became a celebrity.

When I first met him, I did not know who he was. He approached me with confidence and introduced himself. Because he was funny, I gave him my number. He soon became my boyfriend and my best friend. I shared a house with my roommates at the time, and Eric did not stay at his apartment. He was always at my place, so I suggested we get a bigger apartment and move in together, and he agreed.

We always found something to laugh about. We would get up in the middle of the night and start telling each other jokes that one of us had forgotten to tell the other before we went back to sleep.

I did not like partying or going to the clubs. Eric did, and I was okay with that. That's what he enjoyed doing, and I wasn't going to nag him about it. I had the best of both worlds: my time alone and Eric when I needed him around.

In addition, if there was ever an event or concert where a local or international artist was performing and I wanted to go, he would take me. Even if it wasn't his thing, he would still go with me anywhere I wanted him to take me.

I was in love with Eric; to an extent, I was obsessed with him. Everything about him was perfect to me, except at times he could be a bit of a narcissist—but Eric did not know that I had some of those tendencies, too.

After living with Eric for about two years, he called me at work on Valentine's Day and told me that he had something for me. He went on to give me a clue: It had ten letters, and I was going to love it so much. I was excited. I was sure he was going to propose to me on Valentine's day. After all, the word "engagement" has ten letters in it. I could not wait to get home—I thought I was going to be engaged to the man I loved.

But to my surprise and disappointment, Eric handed me a photograph of himself that said, "I love you" (yes, the word "photograph" has ten letters). It was like he believed he was

God's gift to me. I was so disappointed. I could not understand why the man I lived with had given me a photograph of himself. He was disappointed that I was not more excited about his gift.

The photo did not say, "I love you, Melinda." It just said, "I love you." I concluded that he had multiple copies made so he could distribute them to his fans. Apparently, he believed I was only one of his fans.

The last straw was when he came home with one of Jamaica's national newspapers and excitedly showed me that he was featured in an article with nineteen other Jamaican male celebrities who were bachelors. It was titled "Jamaica's 20 Most Eligible Bachelors."

I was upset! I thought, *Here I am, playing a wife's role. I always make myself look attractive for you. I go to the gym every day to keep myself up (even on days when I don't feel like it). I try to be my best self physically. I make myself ready when you want to make love, cook your dinner, clean up after you. Here I am taking care of you, and you are basking in your bachelorhood. You gave me a photograph of yourself for Valentine's instead of an engagement ring.*

I was livid, but I remained calm. I had learned well from the men in Tivoli. I decided that I was going to show Eric that I could do way better than him—I would find another man who had double what Eric thought he had.

That wasn't going to be hard. Men like Eric were always attracted to me, and I already had the ideal person in mind.

I was twenty-five years old, and Terrel was in his late thirties. He was a professional engineer who traveled the world working on cruise ships. Terrel was tall, chocolate-dark, and handsome. He was confident, he had more money and a newer car than Eric, and he had his own place.

Terrel had decided that he wanted to take a break from the sea and traveling, and so he was employed as an engineer at a power plant. He was the ideal bachelor. He had been showing interest in me for a while, but I was already committed to Eric, so I had not responded. But when Eric started acting as if he were God's gift to me, I changed my tune. Now I just wanted to prove I could do better; my ego would not let me take Eric's crap.

So, I started going out with Terrel. Terrel was fun, and soon I was no longer obsessed with marrying Eric. I was too busy having fun spending time with Terrel, going to the movies or to Devon House Park for ice cream or just hanging out at his home.

Terrel and I were happy in each other's company. Terrel knew I wasn't going to leave Eric, and he seemed okay with it, because he too had someone else. I never had any problem with that. I liked Terrel a lot, but I was in love with Eric. It seemed my soul was tied to Eric's, and I didn't want that tie loosened. After all, I thought Eric was going to be my guy forever.

No matter how late I stayed out with Terrel, Eric didn't know, because he came in later than I did. Everyone was happy, I thought. Eric and I loved each other, and I stopped expecting him to propose—after all, what reason did I have to be married now? I was delighted in my love triangle.

One Saturday, Eric and I were home chilling and watching television when my phone rang. I looked and saw that it was Terrel. Terrel had gone out of town for a couple of days and was on his way back and wanted to see me.

I could not just let it ring and not answer. *Eric would be suspicious*, I thought. I answered the phone, hoping that by my tone he might know that Eric was home.

"Hello, who is this?" I said.

"What's going on, my life—I miss you," Terrel's voice echoed throughout the apartment.

Eric looked at me; he was so stunned. "Melinda, did that person just called you 'his life'?"

I tried to find a word that rhymed with "life," but the only word I could think of was "wife," and that was not going to work, so I nervously smiled and said, "Oh, that's just my friend Terrel. He likes to play around."

Eric was already suspicious based on how I had answered the phone.

Eric pretended to be calm. "He jokes around by calling you 'his life'? Come on, Melinda, tell me the truth, what is going on?"

So, I told him that Terrel and I were more than just friends.

Not only did I break Eric's heart, I could see that I hurt him to the core—it seemed I had fragmented his soul. I had wanted to prove a point to Eric, but I had never wanted to go and break him.

He wept as if I had just ripped out his heart. I felt bad for him, but another part of me didn't. I tried to justify myself in my mind. *Well, he tried to break me first.*

Eric told me that he stilled loved me and wanted us to work on our relationship, but, of course, he wanted me to stop seeing Terrel. I figured that Terrel might not want to just let me go that easily—after all, we had a good thing going on.

I was right.

Eric called Terrel and told him that he and I were having some issues and that we were going to work on our relationship. He said he wanted Terrel to stop communicating with me.

Terrel told Eric he could not do that because he too was in love with me.

To say I had a problem was an understatement.

I, too, was wondering, *At this point, can I just stop seeing Terrel?* I didn't want to hurt Terrel either—I cared about his feelings, too. He and I had been going out for several months by now.

But Eric had my heart, and I promised Eric that I would stop seeing Terrel. I asked Terrel not to call me at home. I said I was going to try to fix my relationship with Eric. Although I liked Terrel a lot, I had to choose, and I chose the man I loved: Eric.

All this took place a few weeks before Christmas.

On Christmas Day, Eric and I were home chilling. The phone rang. Eric looked at the phone, and then he looked at me, saying, "Didn't I ask you to stop!"

He snapped and ran into the kitchen for the knife. I ran out of the house, and Eric came out behind me with the butcher knife. I took off.

(Thank goodness for my experience in high school as a sprinter on the track and field team. When I say I took off, I *took off!*)

While running, I remembered to call on Jesus. I said, "God, please don't let him kill me."

Immediately Eric stopped running behind me and shouted, "Don't you see how much you are hurting me! I am not going to kill you; I am going to kill myself and let you have to live with that for the rest of your life!"

I was relieved, thinking, *Well, better you than me.*

Then the neighbors in our apartment complex came out to calm him down.

I decided that since God had saved my life, it only made sense to serve him at that point. Some ladies came to my apartment and handed out tracts and invited me to their church. I was trying to do the right thing with Jesus, and these people came along. I was still living with Eric, but I got baptized one night at the beach. I knew then I had to either get married or move out.

As time went on, I came to understand this church to be more like a cult. The group assigned me a "sister." I thought she was my confidant and support.

I slept with Eric, and I felt terrible for fornicating. *I have sinned against God and myself,* I thought. I told my "sister" and asked her to pray for me. She agreed.

That weekend, the church leaders invited me to what I thought was a house party with about twenty people in attendance. Everyone gathered around a table.

Then the leader said, "Melinda, we are here because we heard you fornicated."

Stunned, I looked in the leader's eyes and said: "Wait, what? Are you telling me that I am called here for that? First, let me make this clear: I am an adult. I sinned against God, and only God, and I owe no one an explanation. I answer to no man or woman."

They were surprised; they did not know I was so forward, because I usually have a quiet temperament.

"Secondly," I continued, "I thought when I told the 'sister' about my being with my boyfriend, that it was in confidence, and I asked her to help me to pray for strength to resist. And thirdly, if you guys had told me you wanted to meet and pray with me about my sin, I would have gladly come, because I want to do the right thing. But you guys are dishonest, lying about the reason why you invited me here in the first place."

They were all quiet and said nothing more.

I left that congregation because I realized that I had joined a cult and they were not ready for me. In this cult, they told the members who to date and marry and how to live their lives.

At the same time, I moved out of the apartment with Eric because I wanted to be a Christian for real. *God has saved my life again and has been so good to me. This time I am going to do the right thing,* I thought.

I wanted to serve God, and I knew my relationship with Eric was irreparable. But it was hard for me to get over losing what I thought I wanted, and I wanted Eric. I still visited Eric every now and then—it was hard to get him out of my system—but things were not the same.

I just wanted my life to work. So many things were not going well. At my job, they promised me a promotion, and I worked hard—but they gave the job to one of their friends. I was devastated, I cried, I felt so betrayed. I also needed a car; I was tired of taking the bus, which is so stressful in

Jamaica. I wanted a visa so I could travel to the U.S. like my friends. I thought that would probably make me feel better about myself.

Eric eventually started seeing other people without caring if I found out, and of course he had no reason to hide it from me. So, I stopped visiting him. I wanted a husband, and he was not ready for that type of commitment. My pride would not allow me to settle for being his "other chick" as much as it felt unbearable at the time. I left for good—my ego was finally far greater than my desire for Eric.

# God Is Merciful

*Precious Lord, take my hand, Lead me on, let me stand. I am tired, I am weak, I am worn. Through the storm, through the night, lead me on to the light. Take my hand, precious Lord, lead me home.*
—Thomas A. Dorsey

I was single again, and life was not treating me well. The Student Loan Bureau kept calling me to repay the student loans I took out to attend UTech. I could not get a good job that paid me well, so I could not pay my bills, much less my student loans.

I moved so many times, I lost count. Even though I had the house in Waterford, I returned to it as my rest stop when things didn't work out, but as soon as I got a chance, I left again. I never wanted to go back. It was my dream to own my own home, but I could hardly pay my rent, especially after Eric and I broke up.

I returned to Waterford for a while. My sister and her children, as well as my uncle, stayed in the house, too. I missed being on my own, so within a few months I had saved enough to move out of Waterford into an apartment of my own.

I wasn't the party or club type. But one evening on a holiday weekend, I was single and home alone. This got me thinking. *I am a nice girl, I don't smoke, drink or do bad things.* I decided, *I am going out—it's a holiday.*

I called two of my girlfriends who were also single, and we decided to go out together. Of all the places we chose to go, we ended up in a "freaky club" with live sex shows. As we walked into the club, it was so crowded we had to take baby steps to move forward, and people were pushing and shoving. The club was dark, with just enough light to see what looked like small caves. A laser light randomly shone on a naked man or woman, and there was a young lady with a dog leash around her neck and a chain. Two couples were having sex on what looked like a stage.

I began to think, *Oh my gosh, this is hell.*

Then I heard a loud voice say to me, "Get out!"

I thought it was God himself telling me to get out. But I was with some of my girlfriends, and not wanting to seem uncool, I kept walking into the club, trying to get to the front of the stage.

Once again, I thought, *This is what hell looks like.* I can't explain it, but for a second it seemed like that's where I was walking.

The place was so packed that even if I wanted to leave, it would take a couple minutes to get back out. The next thing I knew, I felt a big hand grab the back of my shirt and pull me out of the club. My friends did not see the hand, but they did see me running out of the club.

I remained calm. I didn't want to be the weird friend, so when they asked me why I ran so fast out of the club, I just told them, "That place is Sodom and Gomorrah, and I don't want to be in there."

They agreed that the club was a bit much, and one of my friends recommended that we go to an exotic club in Kingston that she said was "much nicer." At this point I was ready to go home, but since I wasn't the driver and I was the one who had suggested that we go out, I went. I was uncomfortable in that club, too, so I said, "I don't want to watch naked women dancing. Let's go." We left.

After this experience, you might think I would decide to serve Christ. No! I was still living in sin, but God was always faithful to this sinner. He loved me when I wasn't loving myself. He never gave up on me. No, Jesus did not treat me with disdain—he showed me love, grace, and mercy. Jesus did not throw me away. Jesus did not throw this clay away, hallelujah. Thank you, Jesus!

### JEHOVAH-RAPHA—JEHOVAH, MY HEALER

Once again during my time of waywardness, I found myself in awe at the mercy of God. Women, please get your pap smears and do your breast exams. Men, please do your prostate exams. It can save your life. Jesus healed me when I never knew I was sick and gave me a brand-new cervix.

I had allergies, and I went to my doctor for a prescription to ease the nagging symptoms. My doctor was not in that day, so I saw a new doctor. She insisted that I do my pap smear that day, even though I told her that I never had the money for the test and that I was not visiting for that.

This doctor decided that she was going to do it for free or that I could pay her some other time, so I did the test. The results came back, and there was a problem. She recommended that I do some other tests, and those tests, called CIN 1 and CIN 2, also came back with "problems." I was referred to the University of the West Indies Hospital to have the problems removed and treated.

Back at home, I was about to cry. I said to God, "My son is just seven, and I am only twenty-seven, and I am going to die." I also thought, *Wow, CIN 2 sounds like "SIN 2"—is that my level of sin?*

I tried to cry, but tears would not come. Then I heard a Voice, almost audible, say in *patois*, "My girl, you are not going to die. Go find a comedy to watch and get something to laugh about."

"Okay," I said. I prayed and asked God for a new cervix.

I made the appointment to have the cervical dysplasia treatment. While I was on the table to have the procedure, I saw in my spirit that Jesus had come to see me there. He took me to the beach, and we walked and talked. When my spirit returned to the operating table, the procedure was done. The doctor looked at me and said, "You don't let no one tell you that you cannot take the pain." I thought to myself, *What pain?*

"I wasn't even here; I am just coming from the beach, where Jesus comforted me" I said. It seemed that Jesus had borne my pain.

> *That it might be fulfilled which was spoken by Esaias the prophet, saying, Himself took our infirmities, and bare our sicknesses.* —MATTHEW 8:17

After a couple of days, I went back for a checkup, and the doctor showed me a picture of my cervix. "It looks like you have a brand-new cervix," she said.

I smiled because I knew God had answered my prayers for a new cervix. It has been seventeen years since then, and—all glory to God—every year my pap smear result comes back normal.

God used that doctor so I could get medical attention, even before I knew I was sick. Hallelujah!

My friends, please go get your annual tests. It may save your life. Take the best care of yourself. You service your cars and clean your homes. You get termite control to spray your yards and houses. You accept salvation for your souls. *Please* check your body from head to toe. Take care of your body—the Holy Spirit lives there, and it's the only one you get.

Go do what is best for your health, body, and mind, and if something needs correcting, trust God—it will be corrected. But the earlier it is caught, the better the chances are of it getting fixed. God bless that doctor and all doctors.

I trust God, and I believe in divine healing. I also know that he uses doctors to heal, too!

### JEHOVAH-JIREH—MY PROVIDER

One day when I was in a taxicab, I saw a calf run out of the bushes into the road, and then it jumped onto a car. It was unbelievable. I had no idea this bizarre event I witnessed would connect me to one of my future best friends.

When I was released after a restructure at the company I worked for, the HR consultant encouraged me to go and study human resources. He thought I would excellent in that field. I met Natasha at the university; she was pursuing the same human resources management diploma. One day when I saw her car, I told her about the day that I saw a calf jump out of the bushes and onto a car that looked like hers. We had a good laugh when we realized Natasha's car was the actual car. It so happened that Natasha also lived in Portmore.

We bonded and developed a great friendship. When I was low on groceries, she shared what she had with me. We looked out for each other and made each other laugh. I did not have a car at the time, and Natasha, in her kindness, would help me get Alex around and take me to and from work, as we both eventually started working at the same place. God bless her! Talk about God providing by sending a ram in the bush—or a calf jumping out of the bush!

Many times, I saw God repeat miraculous provision in my life, just like he had done for Moses. I always had the faith that one day things must get better! Besides, God had already told me that my life would get better if I did not give up.

I held onto those words, and for some reason, when I was going through trouble, I always thought of Job and would tell myself Job had gone through worse. Over time, things did improve for me.

Even though I was not a Christian at the time, Jesus Christ had been faithful to me. I got my dream car, a new, shiny, fully loaded, silver Honda Accord, and I bought a newly built house in a gated community. I got a job that paid me over one million Jamaican dollars per year, plus additional benefits. Alexander fully supported our son financially; things had greatly improved for him as well. He had gotten a job with an overseas company managing one of their departments, so he emigrated. My son and I traveled to the US on vacation whenever we felt like it.

I had never put much thought into how far I had come, from having nothing to having plenty. One day my sister Marsha and I were having a discussion, and she said, "Mel, you are truly blessed. You have a nice car that is fully paid. You travel to the USA whenever you feel like it. You have a new house being built and don't have to worry about paying a mortgage because Alexander takes care of his son financially. You got fired from your job, and within two weeks you got a better paying job!"

I chuckled and said, "Yes, it is true! God is good, and if anyone troubles me, they end up dead or something bad happens to them."

Confused, Marsha replied: "Mel, do you think God would kill someone?"

I had never thought about it before, but I laughed and jokingly said, "Of course—when God said do not touch the Ark, you think he was joking?" I was talking about the Ark in 2 Samuel 6:7 —where Uzzah died after touching the Ark. We both laughed. But after that talk, I kept on thinking about what Marsha had said.

### JEHOVAH-SHAMMAH—YOU ARE WITH ME

At the time I was working with one of the top radio stations in Jamaica as the senior executive assistant to the managing director. I recall one of my coworkers saying to me, "Melinda, be careful of the managing director, because he works *obeah*" (voodoo priests).

I didn't know how true that was, but I knew he did not like me. One of his mentors jokingly told me one day that his mentee—my boss—attended the "church of Satan." I blew it off, as I thought he was joking.

Even though the managing director had hired me as his assistant, we did not get along. It seemed our spirits did not mesh. He was a tyrannical manager, and I was the subordinate who was not afraid of him. (The board eventually fired him.)

This managing director wanted to fire me, but for some reason he didn't want to fire me himself. He would get angry and shake when I got near him. Once he came into my office and started shouting at me. I did not answer him but instead turned my back to him.

I was so upset, I told my assistant, "The next time he shouts at me, he is going to drop right in front of me and die!" My assistant went and told him that. That was funny to me, because now he knew for sure I wasn't intimidated by his outbursts. The following day, when he came to work with a neck injury asking me to make a doctor's appointment for him, I looked and smirked at him.

This heavy-handed boss tried to get the assistant director to fire me, but she said she wouldn't because I was a good worker, so they didn't have any grounds.

I found it strange that he did not want to type the letter to fire me. He finally got his girlfriend to type the letter, and on December 2007, he handed me a letter and said, "Ms. Deir, I waited until the end of the year; it's just not working out between the both of us."

I wasn't the least bit phased. I took the envelope, smirked at him, took out the check, and threw the letter in the bin. Then I laughed at him and said to myself, *This is a vacation; I will be working within the next two weeks.*

He was so livid; he could not understand why I didn't fear him or why I wasn't upset about being fired. I had done a couple of interviews with other companies before receiving this letter, and I knew God was going to give me a job.

Exactly two weeks after I got fired, I got a better paying job with far better benefits. Jehovah, my provider. Yes! He is faithful! Even to a sinner!

The government had to do a background check for that new job because I had to deal with sensitive matters and the government's revenues. They asked why I had left my previous post. I told them I had been fired because I stood up to a tyrannical manager and we couldn't get along. They went and talked to him, but they still gave me the job. He never had anything bad to say; he probably only said that I am a bit feisty if I am pushed.

A lady in my neighborhood told me that two men dressed in black came and asked her some questions about me. I knew who they were; I told her they were like the FBI and it was about a job.

## RESTORED BY JEHOVAH

*What can wash away my sin? Nothing but the blood of Jesus. What can make me whole again? Nothing but the blood of Jesus.*
—Robert Lowry

In January 2008, while driving to Kingston from Portmore to collect my new job offer letter, I was thanking God for always looking out for me.

As I drove, I worshiped God and thanked him for all he had done for me, even when I was not taking notice.

I thanked him for being God (*Elohim*).

I thanked him for being more than enough for me (*El Shaddai*).

I thanked him for being faithful to me; he had never broken his covenant to take care of me (*Jehovah-Adonai*).

I thanked him for providing the new job for me that was going to pay me over one million Jamaica dollars, with additional benefits—after being fired from a position only two weeks prior that had paid me only nine hundred and fifty thousand Jamaica dollars, with no benefits (*Jehovah-Jireh*).

I thanked him for healing my cervix making it good as new (*Jehovah-Rapha*). I thanked him for protecting me when death came to steal me away (*Jehovah-Nissi*).

I thanked him for his joy and his peace (*Jehovah-Shalom*). I thanked him for fighting my battles even though I was living in sin (*Jehovah-Sabaoth*). I thanked him for guiding me and loving me and protecting me (*Jehovah-Rohi*). I thanked him that when he said he would never leave me, he was faithful.

I thanked him! I thanked him for the time he saved my life when I was pregnant. I thanked him for the many times he sent help my way when I was a child without parents.

Then the Holy Spirit visited me in the car and asked me why I wasn't serving him. I felt he had directed me to start going to an Apostolic church in Portmore. I surrendered to Jesus Christ, and immediately after my encounter with Jesus in the car, I went to church. The third week there, I got filled with the Holy Spirit.

A few Sundays after being filled with the Spirit, I was at the altar praying in tongues, and the lady who was ministering (preaching) came up to me and started shouting in my face, "No grave! No grave! No grave! No grave! No grave!" She then told me to continue prophesying in tongues.

My mind went to my old manager. I recalled the managing director had my name and this other guy's name on his list of people to make redundant from the company; he wrote "eliminate" beside our names. The other man whom he had marked "eliminate" died mysteriously shortly after getting a new job: he was electrocuted at work. After all the other things I had heard about the managing director, I couldn't help but wonder if he had cast a voodoo spell on the young man who had been electrocuted, and I knew God had spared me once again. Hallelujah!

Thank God for saving me! With long life will he satisfy me and show me his salvation (Psalm 91). Hallelujah! Thank you, Jesus! Thank you, Father! Thank you, Holy Spirit!

## GOD WIPES OUT DEBTS

A couple years after I rededicated myself to the Lord, I was in my bed when I heard a friend praying. She was crying out to God and asking him to help her. I jumped out of bed and said to God, "If I had the money, I would help her." If I knew where she was, I could at least contact her and maybe encourage her. Little did I know how God would make this happen.

Several years before, I had signed for a credit card for her. The card went into collections. I had just finished paying off my student loan, and I was excited—I no longer owed the bank. I went into my bank to obtain my letter to say that I no longer owed them any money. Instead of receiving the letter of release, I was told that the credit card I had signed for as a guarantor was in default, and I had to pay $300,000 Jamaican.

I got so upset at the bank. I started saying, "I am not paying a dime." I was breathing hard, and I told the lady I had been paying $10,000 every month out of my salary for my student loan. I was happy to finish, and now I had to pay $300,000 for credit that I had never used! I was livid.

In the middle of my anger, God spoke to me. "Melinda, remember you said that you would help her?"

I instantly calmed down. The bank officer must have thought I was crazy to steady myself so quickly. I said to her, as if I wasn't even flustered, "Okay, I am going to pay it."

"Wait a minute," she said. "Let me go and speak to my boss and see if we can work something out for you." She went to her boss and came back.

The lady told me that because I was willing to pay, they arranged for me to pay only ten percent—$30,000. Who but God! After three payments of $10,000, I got my letter of release from the bank stating that I owed them nothing.

I asked the bank office if I could get a contact for my friend. They gave me the email the bank had on file, so I emailed my friend and told her that the $300,000 debt was cleared, and she no longer owed the bank. She was so happy and thanked me.

I told her, "Don't thank me. Thank God."

At the end of the day, neither of us owed that bank. Glory to God!

Another time, I had an outstanding debt of over $100,000 Jamaican because I was careless and hadn't been a good steward of my money. I would take out loans for travel (such as going to New York just because I felt like it) or for pleasure, and not repay them.

When I rededicated my life to the Lord, I was also baptized by water at the Apostolic Church because I did not remember if I had been baptized before in Jesus' name only or in the name of the Father, the Son, and the Holy Spirit. Their rule was that I needed to be baptized in Jesus' name only, so I agreed. It wasn't a big deal to me. (So, yes, I am one of those Christians who has been baptized more than once.) I also decided that I was going to make good on all my loans—as the Bible says, "Owe no man."

> *Owe no man anything, but to love one another: for he that loveth another hath FULFILLED THE LAW.*
> —ROMANS 13:8

I arranged with the bank to start a payment plan. As I drove through the intersection to enter the Portmore Mall on my way to meet with the bank officer, God spoke to me. "Melinda, go to that prayer meeting at the Prayer Meeting Ministries."

It was Wednesday, and the church was having their weekly prayer meeting.

I said to God, "But I have an appointment at the bank. I don't want them to think I am not true to my word when I don't show up."

But I followed God's instruction and went to the prayer meeting. I sat in the back of the church. Then I saw a friend, and God told me to go and tell her something. She was happy to see me, and she said it confirmed the reason she was at the prayer meeting.

Then God showed me another lady whom I didn't know. She had a photo in her hand, and the Holy Spirit said I should go and talk with her and pray for her. I did.

The Prayer Mother (moderator) in charge of the meeting said, "If you have a bill or outstanding debts, come up here to the altar. God is going to clear your debts."

I took the letter I had from the bank, went up front, knelt at the altar, and prayed for God to wipe away my debt.

The Prayer Mother prayed for those of us at the altar. I left the prayer meeting, got in my car, and immediately called the bank to let the person know I was on my way, but I was running late. The bank official said he didn't see my name on his computer as owing anything.

I said: "Look again! I have the letter. I called earlier and spoke with someone, and I am on my way."

The official said he looked on his list, and my name was not on it.

I know Jesus Christ is real, but I tell you the truth: I could hardly believe it myself.

I said, "Have a good day. If you don't see my name, then I don't owe you."

Who but God! Take care of his business, and he will take care of you. I am living proof of that. Glory to God! The Lord is faithful. He is concerned about everything that concerns you.

Shortly after God cleared my debts, I got some retroactive pay from a salary increase. Since my rededication, my new custom, when I come into money, I asked God what he wanted me to do with the money. Abba replied, "Give $20,000 to the elder who preached the first time you visited the Apostolic church and tell him that I love him."

I was willing to provide the elder with the money, but I felt awkward giving the elder cash and delivering a message to him from God. So I put the money in an envelope and gave it to his sister-in-law to deliver.

A few minutes later, the elder approached me with the envelope; I thought he was going to return the money. Instead, he thanked me and told me that he had recently been released from the hospital and owed someone $40,000, and he only had $20,000, and the person was coming to collect their money the next day. He told me that the money I gave him was the exact amount he needed, and for him to hear God saying he loves him was a blessing to his soul. That night I worshipped and thanked God that he saw me fit to be used by Him.

Before I migrated to the United States, I was at my job when I overheard a coworker from a different section telling one of her friends that she lived in a volatile area where guns fired continuously.

I said to Abba, "Please give her a house so that she can move out of that community." The Holy Spirit told me he would, and I should go and let her know. I waited until the following day and then I went to her office.

"Tommy, I overheard you saying there is violence in your community, and I asked God to give you a house, and he says to tell you he will."

Tommy gave me the side-eye as if to say, "Girl, bye." Then she proceeded to tell me about every reason why she was not going to purchase a house any time soon. I got frustrated and left her office. Tommy had a more senior position than I did. I left her office and went to my open layout desk.

As I sat at my desk, the Word of the Lord came to me. "If it were you who needed a home where you felt safe, would you want someone to give up on you so easily?" I recalled how I felt before I owned my own home and how safe I felt living in a gated community.

I returned to Tommy's office. "Tommy, please take the house. God is giving you a house. You don't need to worry about how it is going to be paid for or about getting the deposit. God is going to send help. And if you don't like it, then you can always lease it out. Please take the house."

She agreed to investigate it. I told her about my community, which was newly built and how the contractors were currently building a new phase.

Two weeks later, Tommy called me outside. "Mel, I went to the housing developers, and they told me that a house had become available because the buyer had dropped out. I got it. My family members from overseas sent me the down payment for the house. I went to the bank, and the loan officer told me that she does not know why but that she felt she needed to help me, so she gave me the loan."

I tell you the truth, I knew God was going to give her the house, but I never expected it to happen so suddenly. I rejoiced with her and told her that she got her home within weeks, but I had waited for over a year for my house to be ready. I thanked God as we both rejoiced.

In less than three months, she came to my desk with the keys to her new house and asked me to go and bless the house for her. I did and then returned her keys.

What a mighty God we serve! Hallelujah!

## YOUR TIME WILL COME

After some time had passed, the Holy Spirit said to me: "Look at you now! What if you had given up? A couple of years ago, you were devastated about relationships I never ordained for you. And you got frustrated about situations that were there to teach you life's lessons. How you have learned."

Whatever happens in your life, accept it and learn to forgive yourself and forgive others. Learn to move on—don't hold judgment against yourself. You cannot change it; it has already happened. If it happened, I believe that it was supposed to happen. Take it as a learning experience and move on. Use it to help others and to remind yourself to stay clear from that path in the future.

My advice to you is this. Do not be stressed over a man or a woman you thought would become your husband or wife. Even if that person became your spouse, you might have gotten a divorce, or you might have remained married but been unhappy. Trust God! And love yourself and choose to be happy anyway. It is better to end a relationship than to get involved in a love triangle.

Do not lose hope over a job or promotion you didn't get, even though you may feel betrayed. If you can't travel and take vacations like your friends, don't let that discourage you. Don't lose hope if you can't pay bus fare, much less purchase a car...if you can't pay your rent, much less buy a house...if your health is failing because you are consumed by stress.

Be patient. Your time will come too; trust me. You will love again and laugh again and laugh at yourself a couple of months or years from now if you just let yourself heal and move on. You will buy that car, and you will have that house, and you will be healthy again. All we need in life is to love God, trust him, and seek him and all his righteousness first, and he will give us the desires of our hearts! It may take longer than you plan, but it will happen if you never give up.

# Seek Understanding

Before we get mad at God for "not answering our prayers," and before we question his sovereignty, let us reason with him. He might answer us.

One day I said to God, "You said, 'Come, let us reason,' and so I am here for us to reason." I got two chairs, one for me and one for him (literally), and I said to God, "Please tell me, I don't understand—I have been praying for my mother's healing for almost thirty years. I want her to be healed, and I have been keeping the faith and praying for her to get her mind back and no longer be mentally ill. Even the man was healed at the Pool of Bethesda."

Then God said to me, "You want her to get healed."

It turned out he was not asking me; he was telling me.

At first, I thought he was asking me, so I answered, "Yes, I want her to be healed."

"You want her to be healed," he said. "Does *she* want to be healed?"

Of course! Who wouldn't?

Then he said, "Joy could have been healed a long time ago if she had only forgiven and let go of all the bitterness. Joy needs to forgive all those who hurt her, including your dad."

I immediately thought of the Bible passage that says that if we do not forgive, we will be handed over to the tormentors until we pay our debts, which is forgiveness (see Matthew 18:23–35). *This should be easy*, I thought. *When I see Joy again, I am going to tell her to forgive, and she will be better.*

The next time I saw Joy, I told her to forgive my dad and all who had hurt her. I told her to let it go and give it all to God. She did not answer me. She was silent for a couple of minutes; then I heard her say with anger in her voice, "I will never forgive him; he has done me too much wickedness."

I was sad and said to her, "I am sorry, but you will never get better until you do."

Then the Holy Spirit spoke to me, "She must forgive. She must pray that the bitterness and hurt are removed from her heart; pray that she learns to forgive; pray that her heart is no longer hardened and filled with bitterness and anger. When she is free from bitterness, unforgiveness, and hurt, then the tormentors will have no legal rights in her life and will have to leave."

You see, I had been praying for over thirty years for the wrong thing. What if I had gotten bitter and angry at God for not answering my prayers? I was looking at the symptoms, but now I knew the root of the problem.

Before you get angry at God, talk to him. Find out what is going on so you can pray strategically and fight the enemy from an educated position. God is faithful, and he loves us all. Never give up and learn to forgive. I am still praying and believing. I know it must come to pass one way or the other; with her medication, and prayer, Joy will be well in Jesus' name.

I have believed for over thirty years now, and I am still holding onto my faith. Don't ever give up! Whatever you are praying about may take longer to manifest than you want, but God knows what he is doing. I trust him with all my heart and soul.

In December 2019, Joy told us that she had forgiven our dad and that she no longer harbored bitterness and anger toward him. She smiles more, and the light has returned to her eyes. Joy periodically speak to my dad over the phone and is no longer bitter or anger toward him.

Joy is currently in line waiting to receive her green card to immigrate to America, and with God's help I believe she will be living in the US with me soon.

# Called to Pray

*My Lord, he calls me; he calls me by the*
*thunder. The trumpet sounds with my soul.*
—Steal Away

When I was about twelve years old, lying in bed at Waterford, I heard a Voice from heaven. The Voice sounded like a waterfall with a mixture of great thunder.

"Melinda, come here!"

I got out of bed, but I could see my body was still in bed. As I turned away, my spirit was in the presence of someone great. He was behind the clouds, and I could not stand in his presence. I fell on my knees because of the glory.

*Clouds and darkness are round about him: righteousness and judgment are the habitations of his throne.* —PSALM 97:2

The Voice of Thunder and Water said to me, "Melinda, I am about to do a thing, and many people will perish. But if you pray for them, I will hear you. Pray."

Then I looked down, and there were earthquakes and floods; the people on the earth looked so terrified, running and crying. Full of compassion, I fell on my face, cried out, and prayed for mercy!

As I prayed, the water subsided, and the earthquakes stopped. This has happened throughout my life approximately every seven to ten years. What I cannot explain is that I remember every dream, every time, even to this day.

After I awoke, I felt horrible. (That's the best way I can describe it—it sure wasn't a pleasant feeling.) Since I started reading the Bible, I realized that John and Isaiah had similar visions and that they explained better than I can what happened in God's presence and how they felt.

> *And when I saw him, I fell at his feet as dead. And he laid his right hand upon me, saying unto me, Fear not; I am the first and the last.* —REVELATION 1:17

> *Then said I, Woe is me! for I am undone; because I am a man of unclean lips, and I dwell in the midst of a people of unclean lips: for mine eyes have seen the King, the Lord of hosts.* —ISAIAH 6:5

When my first child was five years old, he was admitted to the children's hospital for over a week. Doctors were not sure what was happening. When they told me the diagnosis, they thought he might have cancer. I went outside, and I started to cry.

Then I heard a Voice whisper sharply in my ear, as if in rebuke: "Why don't you use what God gave to you and see what happens?"

I was confused and said aloud, "Use what? What did God give me?"

The Voice said quietly, "Pray."

I prayed, and the next day my son was released from the hospital. The doctors said they could not explain it, but they ran more blood tests, and he was healthy. Glory to God!

I wasn't even prepared to take him home that day. I went to work; then, when I visited him during my lunch break, they released him in his pajamas. I didn't have a change of clothes for him, so I took him back to work with me in his pajamas. I was working on contract without benefits, so I went back to work so that I could get paid, and a coworker gave us a drive home after work. God is great!

In the first month after I moved to North Carolina, I visited a church. The people didn't know me, and the pastor and some of his team members gave me a word of knowledge that God had called me to be an intercessor. They also prophesied other things to me that cemented my calling.

Several months after the prophecy, I dreamt that I saw myself praying, and when I opened my mouth, fire came out and burned through the ceiling; then it burned through the clouds and reached heaven. In the dream, I could literally go anywhere in the world and touch and pray for anyone.

Years later, God would heal my second child. My husband, Ralph, and I (I'll tell our story later) had welcomed my second son Ralph Jr., but my first with my husband Ralph. A few weeks after he was born, he developed an umbilical hernia. I was a bit concerned because it was getting bigger, like a big lemon, and his pediatrician was stating that he might need to have surgery to get it fixed. I started declaring the words of my Lord and Savior, Jesus Christ, over him. I gained peace from Psalm 138:8: "God will perfect that which concerneth me."

> *The LORD will perfect that which concerns me; Your mercy, O LORD, endures forever; Do not forsake the works of Your hands.* —PSALM 138:8

One afternoon the baby and I went to take a nap, and while I slept, I saw a person who looked like a doctor come into my bedroom. I could not see his face. He went over to the baby's crib, pulled open his belly button, let out some air, and then closed the baby's belly button. Then he said to me, "Your baby is perfect and will not need any surgery."

When I woke up, my little one's belly button was flat as a penny and showed no sign of a hernia. Glory to God!

I have many more testimonies of God's goodness. When he uses me to pray, people get healed and delivered, so I have decided to walk in my giftings for God's glory.

We all have gifts. What are you called to do?

## WANTING JUSTICE MY WAY

I was fifteen years old and living with my sister in Waterford, who was sixteen.

There was a guy named Bill living nearby whom I hated at the time. (I now know it's better only to love.) Every time he saw me, he would grab my arm and tell me how well he could take care of me and would show me his money. One night I went to the shop, and he saw me.

He grabbed my arm, took out a stack of cash, showed it to me, and said, "Do you want money? Be my girl, and I will give you money."

I pulled my arm away from him and went to my house, crying. Of course, the house was dark—there was no electricity. (There was no one to pay for that, but thankfully the house was already paid for.) I stood in the middle of the dark house, crying, and I said, "You saw what just happened. The only reason he could do that is that he knows I have nobody, and if I were in Tivoli Gardens, he could not have done this."

I was so angry. I knew I wanted him gone; a part of me did not care who answered that prayer.

I went to bed. Later, sounds outside my gate woke me. I heard one of my neighbors telling a crowd to move away from my gate, saying, "The only reason you are making so much noise is because you know no adults live at this house."

One of the people in the crowd said, "We are not here to disturb them. We are just here because Bill died last night. He was among a group of guys at a concert when a security guard fired a shot in the air to disperse the crowd, and the bullet caught him, and he died on the spot."

I was so excited, I started to thank God for delivering me from this man. Then I heard someone say the security guard had been taken into custody.

I stopped celebrating and asked, "God, can the judge let the security guard go? Please have the judge say the guy was doing his work and let him go free."

A couple weeks later, I heard someone who went to the trial say that the judge allowed the security guard to go, citing that "he was only doing his job." Of course, I smiled. I felt good. I didn't have that problem anymore.

Even through this incident I learned a valuable lesson: that words have power. Shortly after the Judge had released the security guard who had fired the shot that killed Bill, the enemy of my soul spoke to me; he did not show himself. He spoke as if he were frustrated: "Don't you recognized that you are a witch? Why do you think Bill died within hours after making you cry, and why did the Judge let the security go using the precise words you used to ask?"

I was defiant: "I am not a witch! Besides, I did not ask you to do me any favor. I was not speaking to you. I now know what you do: you send people to upset me, then you act, pretending to help me." At that moment I learned that I had to be careful how I used words and that words have power; I also realized that the enemy of my soul might act on my words if they were not spoken in love.

I remembered the words of the preacher from the tent I attended when I was a little girl, and I shouted, "Get thee behind me, Satan, the blood of Jesus is against you!" He left.

I recall that when I was seventeen years old, I thought, "*It's been a long while since Satan spoke to me; maybe he has left for good.*" It was not until I became an adult that I heard from him again.

Years later, when I was about twenty-five years old, there was a psychic in Jamaica with a weekly program on the local television who gave readings to his callers from his cards. I was intrigued. I wanted to meet him to get a reading.

Eric was out of my life, and I wanted to know what the future held. One day I mustered up the courage and went to see the psychic. I paid $3,500 Jamaican to his assistant. The wait was long, and when he finally came out, he looked at me with deep hatred and anger.

"What are you doing here?" he asked me. "Why did you come here?"

I was puzzled and embarrassed because the other people waiting for him were looking at me.

So, with an attitude, I said, "Why else would I come here? For a reading."

He rolled his eyes and went into his house. I sat where I was. I had already paid my money, so I waited for my reading. I could not understand why he was so upset that I was there. He treated everybody other than me as a welcomed customer.

It was finally my turn. The psychic called me into his house and sat behind his kitchen counter. He told his helper/assistant to cook him some mackerel and dumplings. I thought that he was unprofessional, that he had no customer service whatsoever. I guess we both irritated each other.

He sat on a barstool, and I stood at the other side of the counter. He shuffled his tarot cards, took one out, and said, "They hate you. None of them like you; they begrudge you for what you have."

I was puzzled. I didn't have any money, so who could begrudge me for what I had?

Suddenly, I started hearing clearly. The Voice said, "You know that isn't true. You know you are loved. Ask him who they are that hate you."

I said to myself, "Why didn't you stop me from coming here? You are talking to me now?" I asked the psychic, "Who are they?" "Your family," he replied.

Wide-eyed, lips clenched, I nervously said to the psychic, "That isn't true. I know I am loved. I have known that since I was a little girl, I have no doubt in my mind that my family loves me."

Again, he looked at me and rolled his eyes. He pulled his second card and said, "You are going to have everything you want in life, and you are going to marry a man with money, and he will have a red car."

I was excited until the Voice spoke to me again. "A man with a red car will not be good for you." The Voice contradicted everything the psychic said.

Once again, wide-eyed with clenched lips, I said nothing, but the psychic saw the expression on my face and asked, "What now?"

"Well, I don't think I'm going to be with a man who has a red car." It wasn't my intention to irritate the psychic, but I just had to repeat and obey what I now know was the Voice of the Holy Spirit.

The psychic snapped and shouted, "Get out!"

I remained calm. "Aren't you supposed to read three cards?" I asked.

He said he was finished. "Get out!"

"I'm going to want my money back," I said calmly.

The Holy Spirit said to me, "No, you don't need to get that money back. Go now." So, I turned around and left the psychic's house.

Then the enemy of our souls started to speak.

*"Are you going to allow him to speak to you that way?"*

*"Does he know who he is talking to?"*

*"Say it, and I will make it happen."*

*"Do you know that you could be better than him if you were to do this? He would be working for you."*

I left the psychic's house. He walked behind me, making sure I left his premises. As I was going, my attention was drawn to his little car parked along the fence on the inside of his yard, and I saw in my mind's eye what looked like dark shadows beating or stabbing him. I turned around and looked at him, and he had a frightened look on his face as if he saw it, too.

The thought to pray for him did not even cross my mind. I nodded my head and smirked at him as if to say, "You deserve to have demons beating you." Then, strangely, I said out loud, "Satan, I could never work for you. Look at what you are going to do to your worker."

Little did I know I was already working for Satan, because I had no love for this person. A few days later, they found the psychic beaten to death, his body in a gully. I believed that the demons he thought he controlled had killed him.

# The Power of Love

As a new Christian, I was instructed by the Holy Spirit to go to the Kingston Public Hospital to pray for the sick. I saw a young man who had gunshot wounds all over his body. He was in agony, fighting for his life. I passed him a couple of times, thinking, *He is going to die.*

When I started praying for the sick at KPH, it wasn't voluntary. I didn't have the love I should have had for people. I only went because the Holy Spirit told me to do it, so I felt I had to.

I went to the hospital by myself two to three days per week to pray for the sick. I never felt alone. The Holy Spirit usually guided me to the person for whom he wanted me to pray, and he sometimes gave me messages for people. I did as he instructed, but it never mattered to me if they received the message or not. I had done my part, right? But it was during that season of going to the hospital that the Holy Spirit taught me to love people truly.

*Charity never faileth: but whether there be prophecies, they shall fail; whether there be tongues, they shall cease; whether there be knowledge, it shall vanish away.* —1 CORINTHIANS 13:8

Back to the young man with the gunshot wounds. I was passing him by, heading home, when the Holy Spirit said to me, "Melinda, pray for him."

I stood there at his bedside for a couple of seconds, then thought, *He is going to die. I don't know what to say.*

The Holy Spirit said, "Tell him I love him."

I saw him open his eyes (maybe because he sensed me standing near his bed), and I asked if I could pray for him, and he nodded his head. I took his hand in my left hand and covered it with my right hand, and I said, "God loves you," and I smiled.

Then the Holy Spirit said to me, "Tell him *you* love him."

"I love you too," I said.

He looked at me with skepticism and a bit of confusion, as if to say, "You don't know me."

Then I looked in his eyes, and I said, "Yes, I love you with the love of God," and I meant it then.

He opened his eyes wider, took an intense breath, and then made the loudest, longest exhale I've ever heard. It was a sigh of relief.

Then God said, "Tell him that he is going to live; he has gotten a second chance." I did.

He told me that he was coming out of surgery and that he had to go back the following day because several bullets were still lodged in his body. I told him that he would be okay, and that God was with him.

I went back to visit him two days later, and he was up in his bed. I led him to Jesus Christ by saying the sinner's prayer, he repeated after me, "I believe that Jesus Christ is the only begotten Son, He came down to this earth as God in the flesh and died on the cross to take away all of my sins and the sins of this world. I believe that Jesus Christ then rose from the dead on the third day to give all of us eternal life. Lord Jesus, I confess all the sins that I have ever done in my life. I ask that You please forgive me and wash away all my sins by the blood that You shed for me on the cross. I accept You as my personal Lord and Savior. I now ask that You come into my life and live with me for all of eternity. Father, Jesus – I now believe that I am truly saved and born again."

He told me his name was Ricardo; we spoke for a couple of minutes, and I went away to pray for others. The next Friday, I went to his bed; he was not there. Then I saw him sitting at a window, waving at me. I was amazed: the holes from the gunshots were literally healed, and he was walking around. I was so happy for him. I was touching him, saying, "God was good here!"

He asked me if he was in Kingston, and I told him, "Yes." He said someone had told him that, but he was waiting for me to confirm it because he believed me. He explained that some police had shot him up and had taken him from St. Ann to Kingston.

God told me to tell him that when the police took him to the judge, the judge would set him free. I did so.

I have not seen him again, but I believe he was set free, and I pray that he is still serving the Lord and leading others to Jesus. He told me he would never forget my name because his best friend's baby mother's name is Mel, and I told him I would never forget him because my sister's baby father's name is Ricardo. I left him and went to pray for others.

I have seen so many miracles at the public hospital; to God be the glory.

Some people who were Christians never cared too much for me. They didn't like me praying for them because they said I "didn't look like a Christian, because I was dressed in pants, painted fingernail and hair extension." But the "sinners" who accepted my prayers and God's healing were healed, and I led them to the Lord Jesus Christ. Hallelujah! All glory to God!

# Did God Send You?

*Where He leads me, I will follow, E'en*
*tho' rough the path before.*
—Lou W. Wilson

W hy do I only go where I am sent? I learned my lesson the hard way. When I had just become a Christian, I felt I had to pray for everyone I met whom I thought needed prayer. I hope that you too can learn from my experiences.

*Now when they had gone throughout Phrygia and the region of Galatia and were forbidden of the Holy Ghost to preach the word in Asia, after they were come to Mysia, they assayed to go into Bithynia: but the Spirit suffered them not. And they passing by Mysia came down to Troas. And a vision appeared to Paul in the night; there stood a man of Macedonia, and prayed him, saying, come over into Macedonia, and help us. And after he had*

*seen the vision, immediately we endeavored to go into Macedonia, assuredly gathering that the Lord had called us for to preach the gospel unto them.*
—ACTS 16:6–10

## WHEN I WAS NOT SENT

I was trying to get a professional certification, so I started evening classes after work. I met a lady who was also a student, and during the course, I realized she was in pain. I asked if I could pray for her. I prayed, and the next time I saw her in class, she said the pain had gone away.

She explained that she had been to many doctors and still had terrible pain in her foot. We exchanged numbers. After that day, she called and ask me to pray for her about other situations. A few days later I found myself becoming sick—it felt like the flu, but worse.

One day I was at work, and the Holy Spirit said to me, "Melinda, go home," so I went home (the mercy of God helped me drive back safely). By the time I got home, I was feeling so sick and weak that I could barely crawl into bed.

While in bed, I had a vision. A huge angel was standing over my bed, his head almost touching the ceiling (and my room in this house had a high, vaulted ceiling). He had on silver armor. He looked like a warrior angel with a serious look on his face. He stretched out his huge right hand; I thought he was going to grab my throat. Instead, he pulled something off me. God in his mercy did not allow me to see what it was, but I felt tentacles pulling off me—out of my ears, off my neck, off my entire body—with a popping sound. These tentacles were wrapped all around me as if an octopus had wrapped itself around me. I shouted, "Jesus! Jesus! Jesus!"

Then I got off the bed and looked outside my window to see if I had disturbed my neighbors, but I realized it was a vision. I also realized that I felt better immediately. At the time, I didn't understand what was going on. Later, the lady called me and asked me to pray for her. For some reason, she started confessing that people in her family were fighting over land and making visits to witch doctors and that people were ending up dying. Someone had taken her shoe to a witch doctor, and that was why she had felt pain in her foot.

This lady had told me that she was a Christian, so I thought, *Why was she involved in these things—seeking voodoo priests, etc.?* Then I realized that I was fighting a battle I had no business being a part of.

I said to God, "Lesson learned." I also realized that this woman wanted to take me for her personal psychic as if I could just pray and make things happen like I was God. I deleted her number from my phone, and I decided that before I prayed or entered warfare for anyone, I had to use discernment and, most importantly, consult with God about whether he wanted me to pray and get involved.

I soon forgot about my previous incident and again prayed without asking God if it was okay. Someone asked me to pray that he would get his money back from a Ponzi scheme. I agreed to pray for him. I took the letter he got from the lawyer about his money.

I forgot to pray, and when I went to work, he asked if I had prayed. I told him I had forgotten and that I would pray when I got home. But as soon as I knelt to pray, I heard a sharp-toned Voice say, "Get up! Get away from me!"

I stood up in shock, then I heard, in a sharp rebuke, "Where did he get that money?"

"I do not know!" I said aloud. Then my mistake occurred to me, and I said, "This is the second time, and you should not have to deal with me about this again, I am sorry!"

I went to work and gave the letter back to the man. I told him I could not pray for him and asked him where he got the money. He got offended and told me that he was going to take it to a real Christian to pray for him.

I laughed and said that if he went to a mature Christian, they wouldn't even look at him because they would have better discernment than I did. I also told him that if they were real Christians, they would know that they couldn't go to God with that, because he would push them away, too.

A few days later, this person was talking to me again, and somewhere in the conversation, he began to tell me how he had got the money that he had put into the Ponzi scheme, he stated that most of the money he invested was gained through quid pro quo dealings.

I smiled and said, "Now I know why God pushed me away from your letter."

## WHEN I WAS SENT

As I mentioned, I used to go down to the public hospital to pray for the sick as instructed by God, and he worked miracles and healed many—all glory to God. Every time I went, I would sing, "I must have the Savior with me, for I dare not walk alone...I will go without a murmur, and His footsteps follow still." I was just happy to be one of God's instruments.

There was a man in the hospital who had the worst cut you could ever have seen on a person. It went all the way down his back, and he was crying in pain. I was full of compassion for him, so I went over to pray for him. I did not know what to pray, so I told him I would pray in the Spirit.

I prayed in tongues in the Spirit, and when I finished praying, the man looked at me, eyes wide and wild in shock. I thought he had demons and that they wanted to fight me. I decided that it would be a fight that day because I was not backing down or going out like a punk.

Then he said to me, "You speak Spanish!"

I said, "No, I don't speak Spanish."

He said that he spoke Spanish, and I had just prayed for him in Spanish. He said he felt better—the pain was gone, I smile. As I walked away, he shouted, "Gracias!" God is an amazing God. He is real, and he loves us all. All glory and honor to God!

I saw an old lady who had breast cancer and was going to have an operation the following day. I prayed for her, then stayed and chatted with her a while. But when I was to leave, she said, "Don't go, the young girl who stays in the bed beside me is in the bathroom, and she is in so much pain, I want you to pray for her."

The old lady told me that she prayed for the young lady every night. I was blown away. The woman did not have any family to visit her. She told me her she has two sons; one son was mentally ill, and the other son was unable to visit because he was in prison. And in all this, this precious old saint was praising God and praying for others.

She taught me so much. She had the surgery, and her wound from the surgery miraculously healed within days; she said her doctor was amazed by how fast the cut had healed. God bless her. We both prayed, agreed, and believed that the cancer was cured in Jesus' name.

Back to the young lady: When I went into the bathroom and saw her, she was swollen. Before this day, I never understood how a person could pray for five or six hours nonstop for a stranger. Yet I prayed for her there, I prayed on my way home, and I prayed until eleven o'clock that night. I prayed as if I knew her. I wept and prayed for her life.

I also noticed that this young lady had a lot of faith, she prayed and trusted God even though she was in much pains. The next day I went to pray for her again, and I decided in my heart that if she died, I was going down to the morgue to raise her in Jesus' name.

I went every day to pray for her, and her mother was always there when I arrived. God showed me how to pray for her the nights before I visited her. One night he showed me to hold the soles of her feet and pray for her. Another night He showed me how to make a tent over her, me on one side, and her mother on the next, and then let her mother pray for her. We did that.

After about a week, I went to pray for her, but she didn't want me to come near her. She started saying goodbye to her family members.

When I saw her hug her mom and aunt and tell them farewell, I screamed, "No! You will live."

The doctors and nurses all looked at me. I thought they were going to ask me to leave, but they didn't. I prayed in the hospital until I started seeing chariots and angels in the room fighting for her. I left when visiting time was over. Driving home, all I could say was, "Yes! Yes!" I could see the warfare in my mind's eye.

The following day, while driving to visit her and to pray for the other patients, God showed me a vision of her sitting up in the bed. He told me she would be okay. As I entered the hospital room, glory to God, she was sitting up in the bed.

She told me that the doctors ran some tests and told her she didn't need any surgery.

Her story, she worked at a hair salon and had most of the customers, one of her coworkers gave some food and after eating she became sick. The doctors thought her kidney had gone wrong, but no—God had healed her.

All glory to God. Hallelujah!

*I must have the Savior with me,*
*For I dare not go alone.*
*I must feel His presence near me,*
*And His arm around me thrown.*
*Then my soul shall fear no ill.*
*Let Him lead me where He will.*
*I will go without a murmur,*
*And His footsteps follow still.*
—Fanny Crosby

Father, I will only go where you send me, I will only say what you tell me to say, and when you are not speaking, I will be quiet.

## I CAN NEVER BOAST

A few years ago, I was in my house when the Holy Spirit instructed me to go outside. Then he led me in a specific direction. I followed the instructions until I saw a certain man. Then, the Holy Spirit said, "Pray for him." I was reluctant. I approached the man but realized that he was talking to himself.

I immediately turned to walk away, saying, "But this is a madman, I don't feel like dealing with this guy now."

The gentleman walked in my direction. I walked until I got to my house, and the gentleman passed me as I stopped. As I lifted my right foot to enter my home, I found I could not move. It felt like a hand was on my head, pinning me down. I turned my head, and I said loud enough for the gentleman to hear, "Can I pray for you?"

The gentleman said yes. I attempted to move toward him and found that my feet could move. I prayed for him—it was no fancy prayer—and then he went on his way, and I went into my house.

A few days later, I was in my bedroom when my son came and told me that a man was outside. I went out and saw the man. Irritated, I thought, *What does he want now?*

The man humbly said, "Miss, I just came to thank you for praying for me. Since you prayed, my life has changed; everything has turned around."

I felt so ashamed that I called myself a Christian and had no love for this man, one of God's people.

With fear for the Lord, I said to him, "Sir, please! Don't thank me; it is all God! I had nothing to do with it."

Father, I humble myself, and I repent even today for not loving your people as I should. I will feed others and pray for them and follow your commands as you instruct me to do. Abba, please teach me to love genuinely. In Jesus' name, I pray. Amen.

# My Deliverance Experience

*Amazing grace (how sweet the sound) that saved a wretch like me! I once was lost, but now am found, was blind, but now I see. Through many dangers, toils, and snares I have already come: 'tis grace has brought me safe thus far, and grace will lead me home.*
—John Newton

One Sunday, the lead intercessor came to me after church and told me that I had been called as an intercessor. (This was a confirmation to me; I had known this since I was a child.)

She also told me that I needed deliverance, and we arranged to meet at the church the following Saturday. Now, I didn't know that I needed deliverance, and I was a bit offended—after all, I was filled with the Holy Spirit, God spoke to me, I spoke in tongues, I prayed for people, and they were being delivered. But I agreed to meet her at the church. She instructed me that first I should repent of all my sins.

So, I went home and repented of everything I could remember and asked God to bring to memory anything else I might have forgotten. I recalled the guy who got shot at the "Sting" concert, as well as the psychic. I said, "I didn't trouble them; they troubled me, and besides, the first guy deserved to die because he was a pest to me, and the second one took my money and ran me out of his house; his customer service was terrible."

Then, like a trance or vision, I found myself in Jude 1:9 when Michael told Satan, "The Lord rebuke you!" But instead of talking to Satan, Michael was in my face talking to me. It felt so real that I jumped back and found myself in my room again.

I repented wholeheartedly, and then the Holy Spirit said to me, "Did you know that you could have prayed for God to save that psychic, and he would have been one of the best pastors in Jamaica today? Many other Christians prayed for his demise, too; they should have prayed for him to live! *Who are you* to judge and condemn someone to hell?" "If a person dies in his sin, you know that person is going to hell, yet still, you pray for death upon them! Every soul is important to me" (Yes, sometimes God gets rough with me.)

I repented for seeking a psychic and for everything I could remember and for everything I might have forgotten I had done.

*I take no pleasure at the end of anyone, declares the Sovereign Lord."* —EZEKIEL 18:32

*But if the watchman sees the sword come, and blow not the trumpet, and the people be not warned; if the sword come, and take any person from among them, he is taken away in his iniquity; but his blood will I require at the watchman's hand.* —EZEKIEL 33:6

Following through on the lead intercessor's recommendation that I needed deliverance, I planned to meet with her at the Apostolic Church that Saturday, but my car would not start (even though it was always reliable). The following day it started, and I went to Sunday service. I saw the lady. She told me she waited for me, and I did not show up. Because I did not have her number to call her, I was a no-show.

A few weeks later, I heard on my radio that a deliverance minister was in town, and the Holy Spirit told me that I needed to go to that minister. (So perhaps the first person was not God's plan for me.) I was a bit reluctant. I asked, "Why? Why don't you deliver me now, right here? Too many people will be there, and they are going to see me falling and all the things I see happening to people who get delivered. And by the way, wasn't this man caught up in some controversy?"

The Holy Spirit replied, "What he did is between him and me. That is not your business."

I said, "Sorry, Sir; I will go."

So now the lead intercessor from my church and the Holy Spirit had confirmed that I needed deliverance.

I went, but I didn't want to be conspicuous sitting up front, so I sat in the middle. They had set up video cameras and a sound system. (At that time, I was full of pride, and all I could think of was that I would be seen by the world getting deliverance, and people would see me on the floor doing what people who had demons do.)

This visiting bishop preached, calling out people and praying for them. People fell while he prayed, prophesied, and cast out devils. Then the bishop walked to my row, stood on the seat right beside me, and preached. Then he went back to the front of the room. After a couple of minutes, he came back to my row and called me out, along with the three other ladies sitting beside me.

We walked to the front of the room. There were a few other people there, and he prayed for them. Then he left the three women from my row and me standing in the front for what felt like an hour while he continued to preach.

Finally, he came to me and asked me my name. *Wait,* I thought, *For what? He never asked anyone else their name— why does he need to know mine? Not only will the world see me getting deliverance, but they are also going to know my name! I'm not telling him my name.*

I gave him the side-eye and clenched my lips together. The bishop stood there with the microphone at my mouth; he didn't say anything else. The Holy Spirit spoke to me with exasperation. "Melinda, tell the man your name."

Under my breath, I whispered, "Melinda."

The bishop smiled and shouted over the microphone, "Melinda!" He walked away, then started to laugh and continued preaching and intermittently sang his favorite tunes. All this time I stood there embarrassed. *Now the world is going to see me getting delivered.*

But I had to stay there—the Holy Spirit had told me to. Then, after a couple of minutes, the bishop prayed for me. I did not fall. Then he told me to shout "Jesus" three times. He then asked the three ladies that were also standing at the front to help me cry, "Jesus!" I don't recall him praying for the three ladies who were in the row with me, but he asked them to stand behind me and help me shout, "Jesus!"

The three ladies and I shouted to Jesus, and then I saw what looked like a dark cloud of smoke circling out of me. We shouted to Jesus a second time, and the same thing happened: a dark, circular cloud came out of my mouth. (This surprised me because I wasn't a smoker.) We shouted "JESUS!" a third time, and the same thing happened again. I know one of those dark clouds was a spirit of pride, because from then on, it never mattered to me what people thought about me; I no longer felt I was "the cat's meow" or cared about who saw me getting delivered that day.

While driving home from the service, I was rejoicing and thanking God for my deliverance. Then the Holy Spirit told me, "You need to go back—one session of deliverance isn't enough for you." We had a good laugh, and yes, I returned the following night.

Lord Jesus Christ of Nazareth, Abba Father, I thank you. I love you God; you make me strong!

# Nothing Is Too Hard for God

*Jesus loves me, this I know, for the Bible*
*tell me so...Yes, Jesus loves me!*
**—Anna Bartlett Warner**

E ven though I grew up in difficult circumstances, I dreamt of having a better, more stable life someday. Ever since I was a child, I knew the man I would marry would be either an engineer, an orator, a pastor, or a pastor who was an engineer.

Ralph is a Christian man who loves Jesus Christ—and he's a construction engineer by profession. Ralph was fifty-two years old when we met; I was thirty-five. Ralph is tall, handsome, and very smart; he completed his four-year degree in just three years. Ralph had no children and was never married. I invited Ralph to Jamaica, and he came and met my sisters and Joy. Joy liked him, and my sisters approved.

I asked Ralph when we had just met, "Why didn't you ever marry?"

He told me that he had a friend who had gotten divorced many years ago, and the friend told him that if he were ever to marry, he should think about the ten things about his fiancé that irritated him and multiply each by 100. If he believed he could live with those irritations, then he should go ahead and marry.

Ralph said until he met me, he had not met a woman who met that requirement. That sounded logical to me.

Ralph invited me to visit him in North Carolina. After seeing all he had built for himself, I was impressed. He was a good investor, and I would learn a lot from him later.

Ralph and I married on February 2012. Our wedding day was so much fun! We didn't plan a big wedding; I always knew I would not want the stress or expense of a big wedding.

We got married at a courthouse. Our entire wedding cost us less than $50, including the $20 for the marriage certificate, $5 for the notary signature, and lunch for my husband and me. I never saw a pastor, wore a dress, or had a ring or a cake. We even had to ask two strangers to be our witnesses, but we were married.

After our ceremony, we went to the small café and had lunch; then we went to the park for a walk. I had my dream wedding; my husband still loves me, and I love him dearly. Maybe one reason we are so happy is that we don't have to fight about wedding debts. Ralph was the first man whom I saw kneel and pray to God nightly before he went to bed.

Ralph has a small family: his mother, Wittonia; James, his older brother; and his older sister, Barbara. Their father had passed away several years before. When I met them the first time, I was his wife. They immediately accepted me and my son.

Barbara and I instantly hit it off. She told me I was the little sister she had always wanted. Barbara had been the Director of Continuing Studies at Wilson Community College for over two decades. She was good at what she did, and I admired her. She was a wonderful Christian woman; she loved Jesus Christ and her family. Barbara never got married or had a family of her own, so she showered attention on her extended family, her niece and grandnieces through her brother James, and then Ralph's new bride and her son. When Alex and I joined the family, she always told me it was one of God's blessings. With the additional blessing of Ralph Jr. coming into the world, now they had someone to carry on the Boyette name. I felt that God had led me to their family to bless Alex and me as well.

Through my new sister, Barbara, I saw how God can give us what we do not even know we need. When I became pregnant with Ralph, Jr., Barbara took off every appointment date from work so she could accompany me to my prenatal appointments, even though she was a senior manager at the college with a busy schedule.

Her care extended to all her nieces and nephews. She made sure that Alex and her nieces had all they needed to go back to school. One of our inside jokes was that Ralph had better make the marriage work, because if Ralph and I split, she wasn't going to have another sister, and chances would be that she would divorce him, too. This made us laugh.

## "IF YOU PRAY, I WILL HEAR YOU"

I love my husband. He still opens doors for me. It is always funny to me to see him rushing when we are walking. If I go ahead of him to open a door, he will run with RJ in his arms, trying to catch up with me so he can open a door before I get to it. Then he says, "Honey, let your man do that." God bless him. He's a real Southern gentleman.

Ralph loves being married and loves both Alex and Ralph Jr. When Alex was attending school, if it was freezing outside, or even if Ralph had a cold, he would get up and take Alex by car to catch the bus. He said he didn't want Alex walking in the cold (even though the bus stop is only a two-minute walk from our house).

But there came a time in our marriage when I started feeling overwhelmed. I had a baby, a teenage son, and a new job in a new county (we had just bought a home and moved some distance). During all these trying circumstances, I was away from all my sisters and my mom, and I became overwhelmed. In addition to the usual postpartum feelings, I was feeling the stress of having all the responsibilities of being a "good wife." I believed I was *expected* to be the ideal wife: to keep the house immaculate all the time, to make sure dinner was ready, to have the laundry done, and to always make sure that the baby was happy, on top of having a full-time job.

My husband never wanted me to work; he wanted me to be a stay-at-home wife. He couldn't understand why I wanted to go to work when I had "everything."

He didn't seem to understand how hard a homemaker's work is when you have a baby and no adult interaction during the day. Plus, I needed to have my own independence, my own money to do what I wanted when I wanted.

I know I was doing my best, but I just never felt appreciated. Then I started to think, *This must be a test.*

I was always exhausted. I took the baby to daycare, then I went to work, left work, and picked up the baby from daycare. The baby was still breastfeeding, so I fed him, and then I started dinner and made sure the house was immaculate. That was my daily routine. I also had Alex, and I had to take care of myself. Boy, I was exhausted. And all this pressure led me to become resentful toward my husband.

But I said, "God, you brought me here, and I am going to trust you. I am going to continue being the best wife I can be. Still, I do all that is expected from a wife, but I don't know how much more I can take. I never signed up for this, and I can't do it."

I know for sure my husband loves me, but at the time, I wasn't feeling it.

At the time, I felt my husband did not understand me, nor was he trying to understand. He would say, "You have all you need and want." He did not see why I was unhappy. And if you feel you are not being heard, that can be disheartening.

He has never been abusive physically, and he speaks to me respectfully, and he "helps" with some of the housework. But as humans, we all know when something is not right, and I felt emotionally abused. I felt I was expected to be his version of a "good wife." I told my husband how I felt, but he did not understand. So, I prayed again.

"God, please talk to this man; he is about to lose everything. He has no clue who he is dealing with or what he is up against. I love him, but I am exhausted. Besides, I think this man is testing me to see how far I will let him go. Talk to him, please. I am going to continue being the best wife I can be, *but...*"

I knew I would not take any form of abuse, but I wanted to make sure I did things God's way before I left. Because I know I serve the God who hears!

Not long after, I was in the kitchen preparing dinner, and my husband came home with roses. He often brought home roses, but this time he said, "Honey, I was at work, and this white lady came to me and said, 'Ralph, you have a wife at home, right?'"

He said the lady told him everything about himself, even his past, and told him to take excellent care of me. Then he said the lady said, "You have a good wife at home, but..." and she didn't say anything else. She only invited us to her church (which we visited the next Sunday).

I smiled and calmly said to him, "Jesus loves you, and you need to serve him with all your heart and soul." I told him what I had been thinking, that the "but" meant that I had been going to leave him and that I had been going to take my children, and when I left, I would not have come back to him, and I would have felt justified.

He was shocked.

As I continued calmly, with a smile, I said, "I tried to tell you, but you would not listen."

In that moment he realized how tough I was. He also knew it was Jesus who had sent that woman, because I never knew his location. He works on the road, and he said he had just stopped at a random plaza to buy his lunch, so it could not have been a setup. I was relatively new to the county, so I didn't even know the place where he had met the lady.

God fought that battle for me. Today my husband and I still have our disagreements, like every couple. But he tries harder to understand me, and he does listen to me more, often encouraging me to talk about my feelings. And by the way, he made it clear that he quickly realized I wasn't a traditional wife, so he has let that go!

Let God fight your battles. Be the best wife or spouse that you can be.

As Jesus said, some only come out through prayer. I believe that this was a strong man set up to destroy my marriage, but God stepped in! If the marriage is not of God, it cannot last. But if it was God that put you together, nothing can pull you apart. And even if it is broken, God can put it back together if that is the best thing. If it is not, God will help you through.

> *We know that all things work together for good to them that love God, to them who are the called according to his purpose.* —ROMANS 8:28

When the artist Prince died, my husband and I were watching the news, seeing the artist's family fighting over his estate. My husband looked at me and said, "That will never happen to you."

The next week my husband took us to his lawyer and had his lawyer draft up a family trust to protect me and the boys in case we needed it.

God can put it back together if it is for your good. Just believe and let God fight.

If you feel someone is mistreating you, give it to God! Continue doing good, and let God fight for you. But never accept abuse of any kind. Pray, speak up, and pray again, but your happiness ultimately depends on you.

My friends never give up! My husband, Ralph, got married for the first time at age fifty-three and got his first biological child when he was fifty-four years old. God is faithful. And at sixty years old, Ralph is retired and attends elementary school trips with our son, Ralph, Jr. My husband volunteers his time as a chaperone.

I told him he is a blessed man, because he gets to play all over again and go on school trips. God is faithful. My husband often says that if someone had told him he would have children at his age, he would have told them to shut up.

I also learned through joining this family about the love and loss you can have for someone who is not your blood relative. Barbara was three years older than Joy; she was my sister, my friend, and, to an extent, my mom. We would chat and laugh or go shopping or to concerts. Barbara was looking forward to retirement because we had hoped to go to Jamaica together. I wanted her to visit my home country. I always told her she would love how beautiful Jamaica is. One day Barbara told me that when she was gone not to worry, because God had blessed her by giving her me, Alex, and Ralph, Jr.

We soon found out that Barbara had stage four cancer, which had metastasized just a few months before she retired. Before Barbara passed, she would sleep a lot because of the medication she received to control the pain.

One day she awoke, and she looked mesmerized. She smiled and said, "If I told you about the places I've been and the things I have seen, all the colors, you would not believe me."

A few days later, Barbara made her transition from this life.

God gave me this family that he knew I needed. I love them, and they love me. Abba gave me the best husband for me.

God is amazing; how can I not trust him? I love you, Abba! You make me strong!

# Did I Get a Visitation from God?

*God answers prayer, O soul, believe Him*
—**George Bennard**

During my prayer time in the summer of 2017, I was crying out to God, asking for a visitation. I asked God to come and eat with me, just as he visited Abraham and had a meal with him. That summer, I went to the African American Festival. I took my "boys" (my husband and my youngest son) for lunch, and we sat outside the restaurant. Ralph, Jr. and I ate a couple slices of pizza; then we started chilling.

While I sat and listened to live music, I started looking at the sky, and I talked to God a little. Shortly, a homeless man came and sat beside us. He put his walking stick and traveling bag next to him. There were other seats, other tables, and other people eating, but he sat next to me, at our table. He didn't ask if he could sit with us, and strangely neither RJ nor my husband said anything either—we silently welcomed him. At first, my flesh said I should get up, but I decided to sit right where I was. All this time, the stranger said nothing.

After a couple of minutes, he and my husband started to exchange pleasantries. I was still silent. After a while, I said to him, "Would you like something to eat?" He nodded.

I fixed him a plate of pizza, then went inside the restaurant to get him a drink. I opened the bottle and handed him the glass. Again, he nodded his head (to say thanks). I sat beside him.

He finished eating, then he said, "Thank you."

"You are welcome," I said.

"Why is he telling you thanks, Mommy?" RJ asked.

"Because we shared our pizza with him."

He sat there for another couple of hours. I got up and danced, then relaxed again.

My husband left to take RJ for a walk. The stranger still sat there silently. After a couple of hours, we decided to go home. We got up and left the stranger.

When I got home, the Holy Spirit spoke to me, "See, I came and had a meal with you."

Did you?...I believe you did. Thank you!

Be not forgetful to entertain strangers: for thereby some have entertained angels unawares. – Hebrews 13:2

# God Loves All His Children,
# Prodigals Too

*Sinners, turn: why will you die? God,*
*your Maker, asks you why.*
—Charles Wesley

I am an accomplished executive assistant with over twenty
years of experience reporting to CEOs and other top execu-
tives in both America and Jamaica for large organizations in the
private and public sectors. I have positioned myself to be the
best helper I can be, and so I am a Certified Six Sigma Green
Belt Professional, Certified Administrative Professional, and a
Certified Microsoft Office Specialist. I hold university diplomas
along with myriad other certificates. I know that a CEO is only
as efficient and effective as the help he or she receives, so I
always strive to be an excellent helper.

No matter where I serve, one thing remains constant for an
executive secretary: I must be trusted. This includes being an

excellent gatekeeper/watchman, being privy to confidential matters, having a high level of efficiency, and, to an extent, being a confidant to the CEO on personal issues.

A CEO often will ask me to deliver a not-so-pleasant message to or request a report from one of his division's heads, a director or manager. That director or manager is technically higher up the organizational chart than I am, but because of whom I represent, and because they know I speak on behalf of the CEO, that head must comply with the request—that is, if he or she still wants his or her job. I, too, know that I must follow the CEO's instructions and deliver the messages as tactfully as possible—that is, if *I* want to keep my job. And my loyalty is to the CEO.

I consider myself an executive secretary to Abba; I believe I have done the training, that God has called and chosen me, and that I have gone through the fire and have been cleansed and purged for God's great purpose. I know God has qualified and sent me.

Abba occasionally gives me messages to deliver to a church leader or senior pastor. The difference between my corporate job as an executive secretary and my role as a messenger for Abba is that church leaders usually ignore the message if it is not what they want to hear, and some even get angry at me. Some have gone so far as to call me a witch or to say I have a demon in me. They've called me other names for delivering such messages. After all, they don't know me, and they believe they are higher up Jesus' organizational chart, and I am a nobody in their eyes.

Unfortunately for those pastors or church leaders, the consequences for them are like what happens to a director who ignores the request of the CEO of a corporation. Jesus Christ is the CEO of his church, he sends messages to his managers, and if they don't follow his command, although Abba is an "equal employment opportunity employer," he fires at will. (See 1 Samuel 15:10–23, Matthew 15:8–9)

"But, God, I have visited several churches both in America and Jamaica, and they teach the same things; can everyone be wrong?" I've asked. "I understand why these pastors must collect a tithe from a business point of view. People might not give money to *their* church if the pastor doesn't make the people give, though some preachers might use Malachi 3:9 as a manipulative tool—it seems to work. After all, '*Money answers all things.*' How will bills and salaries be paid if there is no money in the coffer?"

The Holy Spirit has replied, "When I set up a church leader I provide. Also, do not look at the numbers and who is doing what. I do not consider numbers as people do. In the days of Noah, many people were around, but only *one* family—only eight people—were saved. You are all rebellious and have all wandered away, gone your own way. These pastors teach human rules as though they are my laws."

> *But in vain they do worship me, teaching for doctrines the commandments of men.* —MATTHEW 15:9
>
> *All like sheep have gone astray; we have turned every one to his own way; and the LORD hath laid on him the iniquity of us all.* —ISAIAH 53:6

I became quiet. I knew too well what it is to be in rebellion, serving myself. I could not judge these pastors or leaders; I was full of compassion for them, because I knew that although God loves all his children, there will come a time when God will cease from asking us to serve him and instead will let us continue serving ourselves.

Then he said, "You do what I tell you to do," and he pointed me to Ezekiel 2.

For they are impudent children and stiff hearted. I do send thee unto them; and thou shalt say unto them, Thus saith the Lord God. And they, whether they will hear, or whether they will forbear, (for they are a rebellious house,) yet shall know that there hath been a prophet among them.

*And thou, son of man, be not afraid of them, neither be afraid of their words, though briers and thorns be with thee, and thou dost dwell among scorpions: be not afraid of their words, nor be dismayed at their looks, though they be a rebellious house. And thou shalt speak my words unto them, whether they will hear, or whether they will forbear for they are most rebellious. But thou, son of man, hear what I say unto thee; Be not thou rebellious like that rebellious house: open thy mouth, and eat that I give thee.*
—EZEKIEL 2:4–8

At first Christianity was very confusing to me. When God told me to serve him, I thought he meant not to fornicate anymore, and to go to church, give my offering, possibly join the choir and the prayer team—those things I was ready for.

But then I realized that, in addition to the spiritual warfare, a lot of the teaching about finance did not make sense to me. I could not understand why a loving God would curse his people if they didn't pay him a tithe. Through his amazing grace, He saved a wretch like me from sin, and before that he gave me a house, a car, and a great job, health and strength; and these people who have been serving him all their lives he cursed for not paying him 10 percent? This teaching did not seem right to me.

Why are Gentile pastors referring to themselves as Jews of the tribe of Levi to collect a tithe? Jesus Christ could not collect a tithe because he was from the tribe of Judah; and aren't we all the seed of Abraham, and isn't Jesus Christ our high priest in the order of Melchizedek? Not because Jesus took a tithe, but because he has no beginning and no end? Aren't we all grafted in? (See Romans 11.) Hebrews 7:18 makes it clear that the old law speaking about the tithe was disannulled because it was weak and useless.

This teaching about paying God a tithe of at least 10 percent gross on all your money was present not just in one church but in most of the churches I visited. Only one of my neighbors, a devoted Catholic, told me that her church does not preach tithes; she just gives as she desires.

At that time, I worked for a sector that made hundreds of millions of dollars by investing, and as the executive assistant, I was trusted to know when the securities were ready to be invested or when to sell and collect on the investments. So, when the preacher said to give 10 percent and God would multiply it, I could not understand why there were poor people in the church. I knew rich people who were not paying 10 percent to the church—they got their wealth through the stock market and their businesses.

Another concern I had was how I could invite people to serve God in good conscience when every Sunday I knew they would be coerced and badgered into giving, even if they did not have it? I only attended these churches because God sent me, and I gave as I purposed in my heart, sometimes more than 10 percent, and sometimes less than 10 percent. I wasn't concerned about what those preachers said about giving, because I knew it wasn't true. But I had compassion on the ones who did not know, and I was disturbed about how this teaching burdened them.

The leaders read that God was going to curse the people if they did not pay a tithe of their money. I heard a minister tell the congregation to give their 10 percent first, even before paying their bills or taking care of their families. "*At least* the first 10 percent gross is God's money," he said.

I went to God with my concerns. "How is it you save people from sin, made a covenant with them to bless them, call them to serve you, only to curse them if they don't pay you back at least 10 percent on their gross income? These people seem to be serving you faithfully. And I know millionaires who are happy, living their lives not serving you. Their money multiplies as their investment portfolio increases and as the stock market booms."

These people are happy and have fun. I know because I used to hang out with them, and I was happy and had fun. We went to the best restaurants any day of the week and the best tourist resorts on the weekend. How could I invite these people to church and have them listen to these nonsensical teachings on finance and then hear the scare tactics found in Malachi 3:8–9? These pastors, however, had never read Malachi 2, where God said he cursed the shepherds for their rebelliousness. I was especially concerned when my boss and some of my friends asked me why I never invited them to church. They wanted to visit, but how could I lure them into this trap? So, I introduced my boss to one of my friends who is a Catholic, and she invited him to her Sunday Mass, and he went and gave his life to the Lord Jesus Christ. I was happy for him, but I was still concerned about the poor who had God but needed money, and I was concerned for my friends who had money but needed God.

God started to teach me about giving and how he wanted his people to give. The first verse he showed me was 1 Timothy 5:8.

> But if any provide not for his own, and especially for those of his own house, he hath denied the faith, and is worse than an infidel." —1 TIMOTHY 5:8

I asked him, "If the poor are always going to be with us, how is it a loving father is going to curse a poor single mother with three children who cannot pay her bills or buy food, but through fear of being cursed by a God who claims he loves her, she takes 10 percent gross to the church and struggles further financially?"

Soon God started to show me several verses in the Bible about his love and how the Apostles encouraged the church to give.

I said, "God, I know you are a loving and merciful God!"

God showed me this scenario: Picture this: you give your child, grandchild, niece, or nephew $100 as a gift just because you love them. That child goes to the mall and buys a pair of shoes and a JanSport backpack and some other knickknacks for school. They spend all the money.

That child comes home and is so excited and starts to thank you and show you everything they got for the new school year. They did not get all they wanted, but that $100 got them what was needed. To show their appreciation, that child bought you a bar of chocolate for $3 out of the $100, which they hand you with a grateful heart.

You look at that child, and you get so mad that you curse that child with a curse because they did not pay you back *at least* 10 percent of that $100. After all, you gave them the money, and it was yours in the first place. What loving parent would curse their child in that instance?

These pastors will lie and manipulate, they will tell you that Abram tithed to Melchizedek, but they will never tell you Abram was tithing the spoils of war, which was the custom of those days after a battle. Abram never tithes from his personal wealth.

> *And blessed be the most high God, which hath delivered thine enemies into thy hand. And he gave him tithes of all. And the king of Sodom said unto Abram, Give me the persons, and take the goods to thyself. And Abram said to the king of Sodom, I have lift up mine hand unto the Lord, the most high God, the possessor of heaven and earth, that I will not take from a thread even to a shoe latchet, and that I will not take any thing that is thine, lest thou shouldest say, I have made Abram rich: Save only that which the young men have eaten, and the portion of the men which went with me, Aner, Eshcol, and Mamre; let them take their portion.* —GENESIS 14:20–24

Jesus Christ the Great High Priest could not collect a tithe, because he was from the tribe of Judah, and he redeemed us from the law through his love and precious blood. Jesus is like Melchizedek, not because of a tithe, but because they both had no beginning and no ending.

Some pastors will go so far as to say there was never money in those days, and that was why God told Moses to let the Israelites tithe grains, herbs, and meat. But the story in Genesis 23:9–16, when Abraham bought land from Ephron the Hittite to bury Sarah, shows that there was money then. I believe that is why a lot of these wolves and the most rebellious pastors do not use the King James Version of the Holy

Bible, because that translation makes clear that money was around in those days. These pastors who collect a tithe are landowners, with their earthly kingdoms, who often boast how debt free they are. Yet Levites were allowed to collected a tithe because they did not have an inheritance (see Deuteronomy 18:2. These rebellious pastors will never tell you about the tithe that Jehovah God told the people to eat and share with the poor, the orphans, and the widows (see Deuteronomy 14:22-28 and Deuteronomy 26:12).

Many rebellious preachers will tell you that Jesus paid a tithe by telling Peter to get the money from the fish, after the tax collectors asked why Jesus did not pay the Capernaum tribute. But we see that Jesus only did this so as not to cause an offense. (See Matthew 17:24–26). Another important fact is that the Capernaum tribute was tax money and was never a tithe. Another set of rebellious pastors will say that Jesus told the Pharisee to continue to tithe, and so tithing is still justified. (See Matthew 23:23.) Yet we all know that it is only through the redemption blood of Jesus Christ that we are redeemed from the Law. And so, of course, Jesus from the tribe of Judah had to support this point of the law when he encouraged the Pharisees to continue with the tithe of their herbs and spices. Only the blood of Jesus Christ of Nazareth redeemed us from the Law.

*From that time forth began Jesus to shew unto his disciples, how that he must go unto Jerusalem, and suffer many things of the elders and chief priests and scribes, and be killed, and be raised again the third day. Then Peter took him, and began to rebuke him, saying, Be it far from thee, Lord: this shall not be unto thee. But he turned, and said unto Peter, Get thee behind me, Satan: thou art an offence unto me: for thou savourest not the things that be of God, but those that be of men.* —MATTHEW 16:21–23

*And you shall eat before the Lord your God, in the place where He chooses to make His name abide, the tithe of your grain and your new wine and your oil, of the firstborn of your herds and your flocks, that you may learn to fear the Lord your God always.* —DEUTERONOMY 14:23

According to the *most rebellious* pastors, if you give less than 10 percent gross on *all* your income, you will be cursed. They ask for additional offerings and first fruits offerings when Jesus Christ is our first fruit (1 Corinthians 15:20). These are the pastors who give their wives and family titles such as "first lady" and "first children," when God tell us that he is the First and the Last. Who are these pastor's wives and children first of? Are they first to Abba's bride the church? God who is father over us all gave gifts unto his children for the perfecting of the saints. And he gave some apostles, and some prophets and some evangelist and some pastors and teachers. What gifts are first lady, reverend, or first family in the church? (see Ephesians 4:11-12).

These rebellious pastors call their congregations their "spiritual children," but they are nothing like the Apostles in the Bible. They rob, fleece, and manipulate the sheep to pay them a tithe. *Is that love?*

Some call themselves "Reverend," when the Bible tells us that the Lord Most High is Reverend and Holy is his Name (see Psalm 111:9). These people do not fear the Lord Jesus Christ of Nazareth; neither do they love Abba's sheep. They fleece the sheep and do not feed them.

I visited a church where the pastor used the story of Ananias and Sapphira. He told the congregation that the husband and wife died because they did not give to the Lord his portion of the money from the sale of their property; he stated that the couple died because they did not tithe. I was saddened by how he could lie so blatantly when the Bible clearly stated that the couple died because they had lied to the Holy Spirit. The pastor was lying to the people; I was astonished by his level of manipulation and mind control games. The Bible clearly stated that Ananias and Sapphira owned the property and could have done whatever they pleased with the money from the sale. They could have kept all the money if they wanted to; they died only because they lied to the Holy Spirit.

> *While it remained, was it not thine own? and after it was sold, was it not in thine own power? why hast thou conceived this thing in thine heart? thou hast not lied unto men, but unto God.* —ACTS 5:4

Not all pastors do these kinds of things, and not all pastors lie about the Holy Spirit. But for the ones who do, their "religion" is so expensive that the widows, orphans, and poor can't afford it. They place heavy burdens on the poor, widows, and orphans. These pastors make unbearable religious demands that they themselves or their children will never follow. Their yoke of bondage is so grave that the sheep are choked.

How many pastors who preach tithes intentionally curse their own biological children, nieces, and nephews when they don't pay them back a tithe? "Pastors" give to their own children, who have their blood, without expectations. Yet they tell their congregations that our Father in heaven will curse the members who do not pay them 10 percent on all their gross income.

> *"If you then, being evil, know how to give good gifts to your children, how much more shall your Father which is in heaven give good things to them that ask him?"* —MATTHEW 7:11

Let God be true, and every man a liar. A pastor who says that God will curse his Gentile children for not paying a tithe is saying that God lied in John 3:16, where the Word said, "For God so loved the world, that he gave his only begotten Son, that **whosoever** believeth in him should not perish, but have everlasting life."

These pastors are saying God lied when He said in Galatians 3:13, "Christ hath redeemed us from the curse of the law, being made a curse for us: for it is written, cursed *is* everyone that hangeth on a tree."

These pastors are saying that the Most High God lied in Ephesians 2:8–9 when He said, "For it is by grace you have been saved, through faith—and this is not from yourselves, it is the gift of God—not by works, so that no one can boast."

God *cannot lie!* His words are true, amen! It does not matter which pastor preach tithes, or how many thousands of people are in their megachurches, or how few are in their small churches. God is not impressed by their numbers or the many titles they bestow upon themselves. Jesus did not take on titles; nor was he interested in trophies.

I focus on tithes because that's my instructions from Abba, and this is where I see a strong hold on many church leaders. I implore them to please repent. They will have to give an accounting of every word they have twisted in the Bible to swindle money, primarily from the uneducated, poor, orphans, and widows. I pray they repent before it is too late. God is already holding them accountable. I am praying and interceding for them, for God's mercy. This message is God's grace and mercy to them to turn from this evil, manipulative tactic. These are the vilest of men recorded in Psalm 12:8.

*If my people, which are called by my name, shall humble themselves, and pray, and seek my face, and turn from their wicked ways; then will I hear from heaven, and will forgive their sin, and will heal their land.* —2 CHRONICLES 7:14

*I wrote unto you in an epistle not to company with fornicators: Yet not altogether with the fornicators of this world, or with the covetous, or extortioners, or with idolaters; for then must ye needs go out of the world. But now I have written unto you not to keep company, IF ANY MAN THAT IS CALLED A BROTHER be a fornicator, or covetous, or an idolator, or a railer, or a drunkard, or an EXTORTIONER; WITH SUCH AN ONE NO NOT TO EAT.* —1 CORINTHIANS 5:9-11

*The wicked walk on every side, when the vilest men are exalted.* —PSALM 12: 8

Please teach as Jesus teaches, and please teach how the true Apostles taught in the Bible on giving under the new covenant. Please, sir! Please, ma'am! Jesus wants to save you. Please don't be the prophet who did all the miracles, signs, and wonders, preached the Word, even saved people's souls from hellfire, only to be told by Jesus to go away because he never knew you. Oh, what "weeping and gnashing of teeth, when ye shall see Abraham, and Isaac, and Jacob, and all the prophets, in the kingdom of God, and you yourselves thrust out" (see Luke 13:28). There is no repentance then; it will be too late. My friends, Jesus Christ is real, Heaven is for real, and so are Satan and hell. Please choose this day whom you will serve. If you know the right thing and don't do it, you are a child of the devil. Those words make my soul quiver.

Don't focus so much on building an earthly kingdom or on your visions and ambitions. Please feed the sheep. Please free the lambs. Please feed Jesus Christ's sheep!

Repent! Jesus loves you! He goes to prepare a place in heaven for you. Only a foolish person keeps tearing down their house. Why do you keep demolishing the house God builds for you so you can make your kingdom here?

Be free in the name of Jesus Christ!

The Lord commanded in 1 Corinthians 9:14 that those who proclaim the gospel should get their living by the gospel. This does not mean fleecing the sheep or telling lies to get money. God will provide—always provides—for his ministers.

Don't you think God can send one person to give a pastor ten million dollars in one year and every year after that? He will lead his people in giving.

For if there be first a willing mind, it is accepted according to that a man hath, and not according to that he hath not.

> *For I mean not that other men be eased, and ye burdened: But by an equality, that now at this time your abundance may be a supply for their want, that their abundance also may be a supply for your want: that there may be equality: As it is written, He that had gathered much had nothing over; and he that had gathered little had no lack.*
> —2 CORINTHIANS 8:12–15

> *Now concerning the collection for the saints, as I have given order to the churches of Galatia, even so do ye. Upon the first day of the week let every one of you lay by him in store, as God hath prospered him, that there be no gatherings when I come.*
> —1 CORINTHIANS 16:1–3

*[Now for] the third time, I am ready to come to you; and I will not be burdensome to you: for I do not seek yours, but you: For the children ought not to lay up for the parents, but the parents for the children.* —2 CORINTHIANS 12:14

*For as many as are of the works of the law are under the curse: for it is written, Cursed is everyone that continueth not in all things which are written in the book of the law to do them"* —GALATIANS 3:10

Come out! Leave the bondage and condemnation of the tithes lie! Allow people to give as they so desire in their own hearts, freely and cheerfully. God came and shed his blood, so we are free from the curse of the Law. Do not put yourself or others under a curse by participating only in part of the Law.

Please, sir! Please, ma'am! Jesus wants to save you. Please stop grieving the Holy Spirit with your lies. Please go back to the time when you felt like David (**"As the deer pants for streams of water"**). Please go back to that place when your soul **panted** for Abba, when your soul thirsted for God and not for your ambitions and status. The world has given you many accolades and titles; some you have bestowed upon yourselves. But to Abba, you are still his little children and Jesus loves you. Pastors, sir, ma'am, if this is you, please repent. *Reset!*

*Come, ye children, hearken unto me: I will teach you the fear of the Lord. What man is he that desireth life, and loveth many days, that he may see good? Keep thy tongue from evil, and thy lips from speaking guile. Depart from evil, and do good; seek peace, and pursue it.* —PSALM 34:11–14

# I Will Keep Following Jesus!

*I have decided to follow Jesus, no turning back, no turning back.*

**—Anonymous**

I recall a dream I had. I was among a group of students from all over the world. Jesus was the teacher, and the classroom was outdoors. We were walking in a huge field with wheat and weeds, both growing together, with Jesus walking ahead of the class and teaching. No one could see his face because he was always ahead of us. No one could catch up with him, but he was close enough that we could see his back, and all could hear him clearly.

After what seemed like hours of walking, I became exhausted. I saw a smooth, round, dark stone, and I sat to rest. Even though Jesus was ahead of us, he still knew what each of his students was thinking and doing. He stopped teaching, walked back to me, and said in a soft voice, "Melinda, if you stop now, you will no longer be qualified to be called my son." I thought, *Son? Why does he call me "son" when I am a girl?* Then a thought came to me: *It's not important if he calls me son or daughter.*

I looked up at him—I could not see his face as it shone like the sun—and I said to him, "I will never stop; I am just tired."

He used his hands to gather a handful of wheat, gave it to me, and said, "Whenever you get tired, eat." The handful of wheat was so lush, its color alive and yellow. It was amazing. I thought to myself, *How did he only gather wheat, when the field is full of wheat and weeds side by side?*

I noticed that everyone else in the class was also handed a bunch of wheat to eat when they got weary. Some got more wheat than others (my portion was one of the smaller ones in the group), and I particularly noticed that a black lady from Africa, a white man from Canada, and an Indian man from India got more wheat than I did. I thought, *Maybe they have more work to do on their journey than I do.*

I decided that I was not going to eat too much all at once. I wanted mine to last for a long time, and since I didn't get the largest portion, I picked a grain of wheat off my bunch and ate it. Instantly, I felt superhuman strength; then I woke up.

I woke up feeling like a lion. I got up and started running and praising God for about an hour, and still, after that, I was not tired. To this day, whenever I feel tired, I imagine myself picking a grain of wheat off my bunch and eating it, and funny enough, I always feel better. Thank you, Jesus. I Love you, Abba!

I will never stop following you, Abba! I will never stop!

# King of Kings and Lord of Lords

*God answers prayers. It may not be how you expect,*
*but he is God, and he knows what is best.*
*Be grateful!*

> *As the heavens are higher than the earth, so are my*
> *ways higher than your ways and my thoughts than*
> *your thoughts.* —ISAIAH 55:9

One day my son Alex said to me, "Mommy, I had a dream, and I went to heaven, and it was so beautiful; and I saw you in a house, and you were happy to see me come."

I was excited and jealous at the same time: excited that God might have shown him the future, but a bit jealous that I never had a dream about angels or heaven or the beauty of heaven. All I dreamt about at that time was God telling me of impending doom and that I should pray for people. It was always difficult for me to have those dreams or visions because it would literally drain the life out of me to stand in that presence and hear the Voice of Thunder and Water speak to me. I always felt as if I were going to die—or maybe that I already had died.

So, one day I prayed and asked God to show me himself. I said to him, "You knew me before I was conceived in my mother's womb. You speak to me in and out of visions, but I don't know you—I don't know what you look like. We are friends, but I don't know what my friend looks like." I even said, "I am his mother, and you showed him more than you show me, even open visions of angels you show him. Plus, when you speak to me in visions, it is draining." I said that I wanted to have a good, nice dream too. And I went on praying and complaining and whining about how I wanted to see God!

One night I had a vision. Two angels came for me (dressed like ordinary men—no wings or anything). One seemed to be in training, and the elder one was like a teacher and said to me, "God is going to show you his face."

I got so excited. I said to myself, *This might be it!* I realized that I might not wake up because the Bible says that anyone who sees God's face will die (Exodus 33:20). I was okay with not waking up if I got to see God. The angels took me to a certain place, but I didn't think it was heaven. There were no golden roads. Other angels were there, some with wings, and some who looked like normal human beings. My two angels took me to what looked like the end of the earth and then to a huge tree, the biggest tree I had ever seen, suspended at the end of the earth.

The elder angel said to me, "You cannot go any further."

"Then how am I going to see God?" I asked.

The angel said, "He is going to engrave his image on the trunk of this tree for you to see."

I was annoyed—I thought I was going to heaven to see God and some pretty stuff—so I said with an attitude, "Whatever."

The young angel was shocked at my attitude, and he thought, *Does he allow her to behave like that?* (In the spirit, you can read minds.)

The older angel said, "Don't pay her any attention. He is still working on her."

I stood in front of the tree and saw a huge right hand come through the clouds and start to engrave in the tree using its index finger. It was amazing: the finger engraved with fire and the art was in color. First, he drew a pair of brown eyes; they were beautiful. I got so excited. Then the cheeks, and I could not contain myself; then the golden-brown mane, nicely trimmed (I tell you Jesus is the perfect artist), and I could not stand still. I thought he was painting the face of a man, but it wasn't.

Then he finished the painting. I was in shock. Then, above the picture, he wrote "King of All Kings, Lord of All Lords," and below the painting he wrote "Lion of Judah." I stood in shock. He had painted the face of a lion! I was disappointed.

I said to the angel, "You mean to tell me that you brought me here to show me the face of a lion! And you told me that God is going to show me his face?"

The young angel was even more surprised at my attitude.

Then I heard a still, soft Voice in my spirit. "Melinda, you need to repent."

Then, still in that vision, I remembered another vision I had a while back when I saw a portal opened and I knew Jesus was looking out at me. I saw his sandals, but because of my attitude he closed the portal in my face. I apologized and said, "You never had to show me anything. I am sorry." I repented.

After I woke, I was still repenting.

The moral of this is that God's ways are higher; he is the all-knowing God! What if he wanted to show me the side of him that is also a lion? Like Job, "I am unworthy—how can I reply to you? I put my hand over my mouth. I have said too much already. I have nothing more to say" (Job 40:4).

I humble myself before you, Lord, King of all Kings, Lord of All Lords, Lion of Judah. I must learn to be quiet!

# Jesus Is Coming Back—the Banquet Is Prepared

*How did I make it over? My soul looks back and wonders, how did I make it over? I had a mighty hard time, but I made it over. As soon as I can see Jesus, the man that died for me, the man that bled and suffered and he hung on Calvary. I want to thank God for how he taught me. Oh, thank my God how he kept me. I'm going to thank him because he never left me. And I'm going to thank God for giving me a vision.*

—Clara Ward

A vision I had a couple years ago still puts a smile on my face. I was going into my house when I heard a soft, melodic voice say, "Melinda, look up." When I looked up, I saw an angel hover around me; she had semi-translucent lights stitched all around the inside edges of her wings. Then I saw a window opened in heaven, and I could see with 20/20 vision, as if I had superhuman sight. It felt so real. And in that vision, I remembered another vision that I had a few months prior and I began to laugh...In the first vision I stood, and a portal opened parallel to me. I turned around and saw the lushest green grass; the color seemed to be in 3D and was alive. Five angels, both male and female, stood under a fruit tree having a conversation; these angels did not have wings, they wore a simple white cassock, each had on a different color sash, and these colors were bright and vibrant. The angel with the yellow sash, she had golden blond hair. The angel with the orange sash, she had orange/red hair; the angel with the green sash, he looked Asian; the angel with the royal blue sash, he was black, but his hair looked like an Indian's; and as for the angel with the red sash, I did not see his face; neither do I remember his hair.

I was about to walk through the portal when the angel with the yellow sash came and stood at the entrance of the portal and told me that I could not enter. I was very annoyed, and I asked her "who was going to stop me." But she just stood there with a fierce look on her face. I said to her, "Jacob wrestled with the angel; let it be recorded today that Melinda wrestled with the angel. I want to know if this is real, and Abba knows that that if he opens a portal to me, he knows I am going to go through it." As I was about to run into the angel to see if I could push her out of the way, the angel who wore the royal blue sash came out of the portal and touched me. It was unbelievable! I said to him in shock, "This is real!

I felt your touch." He smiled with the most beautiful smile and jokingly said, "Melinda, you are something else, do you know that?". I was beside myself; I kept saying, I can't believe it! I felt your touch, and this is real! Then I woke up.

In this second vision the portal was opened in the sky and I thought, *"Abba, you do have a sense of humor. There was no way I could even consider entering in."* But I had superhuman sight, and I saw an angel carrying a huge golden harp. The angels were gliding instead of walking, and they moved items with their minds. In my mind, they were preparing for the banquet. Then I saw another angel carrying the seven golden candlesticks, and another angel followed, carrying the high priest's breastplate with the twelve beautiful stones. I was so amazed to see these marvelous things and so excited that I started to shout, "I can see! I can see! I am seeing gold and the beautiful colors!" The angel smiled at my enthusiasm.

Then it started to rain, but I was not getting wet, and I wondered why I wasn't feeling the water on my skin when everything else seemed so real. I realized that it was raining gold dust. I was covered in gold from head to toe, and the angel that hovered above me said, "Melinda, the gold dust is the kisses of God. God is kissing you."

I was so excited! I started to praise God, and I gave him thanks for letting me see these marvelous things and for his kisses. I began to throw him back kisses as I told him thanks.

While I was praising him, I saw demons falling like lightning, but I didn't pay them any attention; I just kept on praising.

Jesus is coming back, I don't know when, but the banquet is being prepared. We all will face Jesus Christ someday, either by our time ending on this earth or when he returns. Based on the choices you make on this earth, he will either tell you to enter in or to depart from him because he never knew you.

*What will you hear?*
*Are you ready?*
*Please be ready!*

I love you all with the love of Jesus Christ!
**Jesus Christ is real!**

# About the Author

Melinda Boyette, a native of beautiful Jamaica, is a wife and mom first, but she counts it her greatest privilege to proclaim the good news that Jesus Christ saves and that he loves all his children. Her good sense of humor and biblically grounded knowledge allows her to share with both believers and non-believers.

Melinda is an author, entrepreneur, and visionary. She and her husband operate their family business, leasing several homes that they own. Melinda is a state employee, a notary public, a licensed and ordained minister, and the CEO of Deir to Dream, LLC.

It gives Melinda great joy to feed her family, so most evenings Melinda can be found in the kitchen preparing meals for her husband and their two sons. Melinda and her family reside in the serene "City of Oaks" Raleigh, North Carolina.

**Visit: www.deirtodream.com**

Thanks for reading, I hope you enjoyed this book. If you enjoyed it, please leave a review on the site from which you purchased it.

Made in USA - Kendallville, IN
1099400_9780578631684
05.05.2020 0855